God's Measure Versus Man's Measure

Getting Free From The False Standard People Measure Their Lives By!

Rudi Louw

Copyright © 2014 by Rudi Louw Publishing

All rights reserved solely by the author. No part of this book may be reproduced in any form *without the permission of the author.*

Most Scripture quotations are taken from the RSV®, *Revised Standard Version*, Copyright © 1983 by Thomas Nelson, Inc.

Some Scripture quotations are from the *Ruach Translation,* Holy Bible, published by Kingdom of Priests Publishing, printed by Graphic Elite with permission of Elyon Word Ministry.

And some Scripture quotations were taken from the NKJV, *New King James Version*, Copyright © 1983 by Thomas Nelson, Inc.

The Scripture quotations not taken from the RSV, and NKJV are a *literal translation* of the Scriptures.

The Holy Scriptures are just that, HOLY.

The statements enclosed in brackets were inserted into Scripture quotations to add emphasis or to clarify the meaning of what is being said in those scriptures.

The integrity of God's Word to man was not compromised in any way. Due care and diligence was cautiously exercised to keep the Word of Truth intact.

Table of Contents

The Marvel of the Holy Bible 5

Foreword 11

Acknowledgment 15

Prayer 21

1. God's Approval Of Us! 23

2. The Fall Of Man 27

3. Justify Ourselves? No Way! 31

4. The Glory of God! 39

5. Death; The Opposite Of ZOE! 45

6. The Measuring Standard Of The Law! 55

7. The Nature Of Sin! 73

8. The Power Of Sin Must Be Broken! 95

9. Our Identification With Jesus! 103

10. The Glory Of Man Versus The Glory Of God! 113

11. There Is No Comparison; No Alternative Will Do! 125

12. The Accurate Measure Of Ministry! 137

13. *Appreciation Always Determines Value!* *151*

About the Author *165*

The Marvel of the Holy Bible

1. Uninterrupted Theme and Inspired Thought

It took *1,500 years* to compile the Holy Bible, involving *more than 40 different authors*. Yet the theme and inspired thought of Scripture continues *uninterrupted* from author to author, from beginning till end.

2. Absence of Mythical Stories

Compare philosophies and theories about creation in the Middle East, Europe, Asia, Africa, and Latin America and you'll find mythical scenarios: gods feuding and cutting up other gods to form the heavens and the earth, etc.

In ancient Greek mythology, Atlas carries the earth on his shoulders. In India, Hindus believe eight elephants carry the earth on their backs.

But in contrast, Job, the oldest book in the Holy Bible, declares that, *"God suspends the earth on nothing."* (Job 26:7)

This was said millennia before Isaac Newton discovered the invisible laws of gravity that delicately balance every planet and sun in its individual circuit.

In sharp contrast to every other ancient attempt to give a creation account, *the Holy Bible pictures the creation of the earth in a very scientific manner.*

For example: In Genesis Chapter One, the continents are lifted from the seas, then vegetation is formed and later animal life, all reproducing *'according to its own kind'*, **thus recognizing the fixed genetic laws.** In addition, we have the bringing forth of man and woman, *all done by God in a dignified and proper manner, without mythological adornments.*

The balance or remainder of the Holy Bible follows suit.

*The narratives are **true historical documents**, faithfully reflecting society and culture **as history and archaeology would discover them thousands of years later. Not only is the Holy Bible historically accurate, it is also reliable when it deals with scientifically proven subjects.***

It was never intended to be a textbook on history, science, mathematics, or medicine. *However, when its writers touch on these subjects,* **they often state facts that scientific advancement would not reveal, or**

even consider, until thousands of years later.

While many have doubted the accuracy of the Holy Bible, time and continued research have consistently demonstrated that the Word of God is better informed than its critics.

3. Intactness

Of all the ancient works of substantial size, the Holy Bible survives intact, against all odds and expectations.

Compared with other ancient writings, the Holy Bible has more manuscripts as evidence to support it than any ten pieces of classical literature combined!

The plays of William Shakespeare, for instance, were written about four hundred years ago, after the invention of the printing press. Many of his original writings and words have been lost in numerous sections, *yet the Holy Bible's uncanny preservation has weathered thousands of years of wars, contradictions, persecutions, fires and invasions.*

Through the centuries Jewish scribes have preserved the Holy Bible's Old Covenant text, **such as no other manuscripts have ever been preserved. They kept tabs on every letter, syllable, word and paragraph.** They *continued from generation to generation to appoint and train special groups of men within their culture* **whose sole duty it was to preserve and transmit these documents <u>with perfect accuracy and fidelity</u>**.

Who ever bothered to count the letters, syllables, or words of Plato, Aristotle, or Seneca for that matter?

When it comes to the New Testament, the actual number of preserved manuscripts is so great that it becomes overwhelming. *There are more than 5,680 Greek manuscripts, more than 10,000 Latin Vulgate manuscripts and at least 9,300 other versions. Further still, there exists an additional 25,000 manuscript copies of portions of the New Testament.* **No other document of antiquity even begins to approach such numbers.**

The closest in comparison is Homer's <u>Iliad</u>, with only 643 manuscripts. The first complete work of Homer only dates back to the 13th century.

4. Unmatched Accuracy in Predictive Foretelling

The Holy Bible is unmatched in accuracy in predictive foretelling. No other ancient work succeeds in this, or even begins to attempt this.

Other books such as the Koran, the Book of Mormon, and parts of the Veda claim divine inspiration; **but none of these books contain predictive foretelling.**

This one undeniable fact we know for certain: *While microscopic scrutiny would show up the imperfections, blemishes, and defects of any work of man, <u>it magnifies the beauties and perfection of God</u>. Just as every flower displays in accurate detail the reflection and perfection of beauty, <u>so does the Word of Truth when it is scrutinized</u>.*

Historian Philip Schaff wrote:

*"Without money and weapons, Jesus the Christ conquered more millions than Alexander, Caesar, Muhammad, and Napoleon. Without science and learning, He (Jesus the Christ) shed more light on things human and divine than all philosophers and scholars combined. Without the eloquence of schools, He (Jesus the Christ) spoke such words of life as was never spoken before or since and produced effects which lie beyond the reach of orator or poet. Without writing a single line, He (Jesus the Christ) set more pens in motion and furnished themes for more sermons, orations, discussions, learned volumes, works of art, and songs of praise **than the whole army of great men of ancient and modern times combined**."* (*The Person of Christ*, p33. 1913)

Today, there are literally billions of Bibles in more than 2,000 languages.

Isn't it about time you find out what it really has to say?

Hey listen, the Holy Bible is all about Jesus, the Messiah, the Christ…

…and everything about Jesus Christ is really about YOU!!

Study Tips:

Read 2 Corinthians 5:14, 16, 18, 19, and 21.

In the light of these Scriptures, it should be obvious that, if you want to study the Holy Bible, *you should study it in the light of Mankind's redemption!*

Feed daily on **redemption realities** found in the book of Acts, in Romans Chapters One through Eight, and in Ephesians, Colossians, and Galatians. These realities are also found in 1 Peter Chapter One, 2 Peter Chapter One, James Chapter One, as well as in 1 and 2 Corinthians.

Foreword

Thank you for taking the time to read this book.

Let me start off by saying that *I am totally addicted to my Daddy's love for me.*

I am in love with Jesus Christ, *and that is enough for me!*

The love of God is so much more than a doctrine, a philosophy, or a theory. It is so much more and goes so much deeper than knowledge; *it way surpasses knowledge.* **We are talking heart language here.**

Thus, I write *to impact people's hearts,* to make them see the mysteries that have been hidden in Father God's heart concerning Christ Jesus, and actually *concerning THEM,* so as to arrest their conscience with it, *that I may introduce them to their original design and to their true selves,* **and present them to themselves perfect in Christ Jesus** *and set them apart unto Him* **in love,** as a chaste virgin.

We are involved with the biggest romance of the ages. Therefore this book cannot be read as you would a novel: *casually.* It is not a cleverly devised little myth or fable. **It contains revelation and** *truth* **into some things you may or may not have considered before.**

It is *the TRUTH of God, ultimate TRUTH, and therefore has direct bearing upon YOUR life.* The Word and the Spirit are my witness *to the reality of these things!*

Be like the people of Berea the apostle Paul ministered to in Acts 17:11. Open yourself up to study the revelation contained in this book **to discover for yourself the reality of these things**.

Be forewarned! Do not become guilty of the sins of the Pharisees, **or you too will miss out on the depth of fulfillment God Himself, who is LOVE, wants to give you**.

Jesus said of the Pharisees and Sadducees that they strain out every little gnat BUT swallow whole camels. What He meant by that is that *some people seem to have it all together when it comes to doctrine and they love to argue.* **It makes them feel important, but it is nothing other than EMPTY religious and intellectual pride.** *They know the Scriptures in and out, and YET they are still so IGNORANT about* **REAL TRUTH that is only found in LOVE.** They are always arguing over the use of *every little jot and tittle* and over the meaning and interpretation of **every word of Scripture,** *but they are still so ignorant and indifferent t***owards the things that REALLY MATTER!**

The exact thing they accuse everyone else of doing though, the precise thing they judge everyone else for, *they are actually doing themselves.* That is **they often downright misinterpret and twist what is being said, *making a big deal of insignificant things while obscuring or weakening God's real truth: the truth of His LOVE*.** *They are always majoring on minors* <u>**because they do not understand the heart of God**</u> ***and therefore they constantly miss the whole point of the message.***

Paul himself said it so beautifully,

*"...the letter kills but **the Spirit BRINGS LIFE**;"*

*"...<u>knowledge puffs up</u>, but **LOVE EDIFIES**."*

I say again: *Allow yourself to get caught up in the revelation I am about to share.* Open yourself up to study the insight contained in this book, *not only with a desire to gain knowledge, but also with anticipation* **to hear from Father God yourself; to encounter Him through His Word, and to embrace truth, in order to know and believe the LOVE God has for <u>you</u>, and get so caught up in it, that you too may receive from Him LOVES' impartation of LIFE.**

The message proclaimed in the gospel and thus also revealed in this book is the voice and call of LOVE Himself to every human being on the face of this earth. *If you take heed to it, it is custom designed and guaranteed to forever alter and enrich your life!*

Acknowledgment

I want to acknowledge and thank one of my mentors in the faith, Francois du Toit, for blessing and impacting me with revelation knowledge.

I borrowed the portion on *"The Marvel of the Holy Bible"* from his website: http://www.MirrorWord.net, as students so often feel they have a right to do with things that come from teachers they respect. Just as Galatians 6:6 says, *"Let him who is taught the Word **share in all good things** with him who teaches."*

To all our dear friends and family, for all the love and support, and to Chase Aderhold and all those who helped me with this project:

THANK YOU!

Also, especially to my wife, Carmen;

For keeping me real by being my companion in life and partner in ministry,

I love and appreciate you so very much!

"Not that we venture
to class
or compare ourselves
with some of those
who commend themselves.

**Bus when they
measure themselves
by one another,**

**and compare themselves
with one another,
they are without
understanding.**

But we will not boast
beyond limit,

but will <u>keep</u>
to the limits
God has apportioned us,

to reach even to you.

For we are not
overextending ourselves,
as though we did not reach
you;

we were the first

to come to you

<u>*all the way*</u>

with the gospel of Christ

*We do not boast beyond limit,
in other men's labors;*

but our hope is
that as your faith increases,

*our field among you
may be greatly enlarged,*

So that we may preach the gospel *in lands beyond you*"

- 2 Corinthians 10:12-16

Prayer

Thank you Jesus that You opened up to us, through the tearing of the veil of Your flesh, *a new and a living way!*

...And in this new and living way, we thank you that we may behold You, *and the glory that You have revealed,* **as in a mirror** *...and that this glory is our portion* **now!**

We worship You Lord!

Father I thank you for enlightened understanding!

...And thus, as we speak Your word, and even as I write, Father, *that Your Word will go forth* **in clarity and in accuracy** *...*so that men and women's lives will be liberated, under the impact of the truth **revealed!**

Thank you Father.

Thank you for the Holy Spirit.

Thank you that He indwells us *and unveils to us* the truth of the Word, *and interprets to us* the hidden mystery of God.

Father, we thank you that there is no barrier to receiving from You *...no language barrier, no intellect barrier ...no barrier of any kind!*

Thank you that we are receiving and embracing truth, *as our spirits combine with Your Spirit* **and comprehend!**

In Jesus name!

Amen

Chapter 1

God's Approval Of Us!

As you can derive from the title of this book, I want us to look at and study together the whole subject of: *"The Measure of a Man,"* and really **God's measure of YOU in particular.**

In one of my other books: *No Longer Looking for Applause,* I explored the concept of *people's hunger for applause and their need for positive recognition* **and the extent that they would go to in order to receive that recognition from other people.** I spoke of how they then used that recognition *as a basis for righteousness; for justification,* and to bolster their ego and feed their pride and silence or soothe their conscience, *and so to justify their existence on this planet!*

You see, every person in their essence realizes, from the earliest stages of consciousness *that there is more to them than meets the eye.* We have all come to realize that there is more to us than just being a part of the rest of the decoration on this planet! We have all realized that there is more to us than just kind of making it through the day and through the season and then to die at a good old age, and hopefully to be able to leave an inheritance to our children and a monument to our good conduct! **We all know, deep within ourselves that there must be more,** *so we hunger and crave for righteousness!*

What I mean is that ***we all hunger for the kind of appreciation, the kind of approval, that would permanently satisfy and fulfill us.*** And let me tell you, *it is no strange thing,* because all we have to do is go and read from our Bibles in Genesis 1 and 2 *and discover how Mankind, every single individual on this planet,* **was created for applause.**

We were designed for approval!

God did not have in mind a being in us *that would be inferior* **and not measure up to His own approval!** We see how God desired to give such expression, such exhibition to His own desire for a being, for people, for us, *for you and for me,* **to be His eternal companion, that He did not leave any of us in any way lacking in glory, lacking in the full brilliance of His design;** *in the full brilliance of His own design.* **He did not leave any of us lacking in the full brilliance of His own image and likeness!**

There in the book of Genesis, in Chapter One, if you study the Hebrew text you will discover there is a beautiful word used to describe *what happened when God first saw His desire come to life in this being called Man.* It says that *"He blessed* (or BAW-RAKED) *him."*

That Hebrew word means literally **to fall upon your knees in adoration and appreciation**

and enjoyment! God blessed him; ***God blessed US!***

God was so overwhelmed with what He saw at the fulfillment of His eternal dream **that He saw and gave and expressed to this Man, *and to us all,* the full approval, the ultimate applause that we could possibly receive and accommodate!**

And now I want you to turn with me in your Bible, if you have it, to Romans Chapter Three.

If you don't have your Bible handy don't worry about it, *just take in what you can.* You can go look it up and study it later, and I am sure you would want to after reading this book.

Ha… ha… ha…

In fact, you might need to re-read this book *and maybe read some portions of it more than once* in order to get the revelation I'm sharing *to settle down deep on the inside of you, in your spirit,* ***so that it might begin to form a foundation of thinking to build your life upon***.

Chapter 2

The Fall Of Man

As an introduction, let me just say that we all should know by now that *the Fall has come,* and how the Fall corrupted this being called Man *and married, as it were, this being, this Man, mankind, to our enemy and to the enemy of everything good that comes from God.* The Fall corrupted mankind as a whole *and every individual as well;* **we were all affected by that corruption!** *And the Fall subjected us to the manipulation and controlling influence of* **darkness**, the manipulation and governmental control of the devil and his forces of **darkness!**

You see, there was a kind of new birth that took place in the Fall, **there was a birth of a new creature. Sin and Man united in one body!** *There was a birth of a new nature in Man, a corrupt nature;* **Sin's own nature. It was nothing short of the corruption of Man's mind and Man's being that took place there! Man became a new kind of creature, a creature that would now be forced to no longer give expression to the Divine nature, to that image and likeness of God that he was made in,** *but to give expression to the lie and the deception he bought into,* **and thus to that corruption inevitably brought** into *his mind and into his soul and into his spirit and his body; into his whole being!*

A distortion of our original design took place!

Our true identity became obscured to us, *and thus that true design went dormant!*

When Adam partook of sin, *when he partook of the enemy's lies and deception* and when he then transgressed and trespassed and partook of that tree; **when he partook of that other knowledge other than the knowledge of God,** he came under its influence, its control; **its power!** He came under the devil's power, under his manipulation and control and strong influence!

You see, Sin was not just some kind of temporal thing, **some kind of temporary conduct! *It was not some little misbehavior that Adam involved himself in!*** **Otherwise Adam could just stop misbehaving and he would be fine. But that initial sin, that transgression, that trespass, opened the door for a link to be established between Man and his enemy, the enemy of our design, of everything truly good that comes from God, and it opened the door to a new birth inside of Man. That sin, that transgression, that trespass, that link, birthed Sin, it birthed corruption! It birthed a new government; *a new government within Man and over Man.* That initial sin and transgression and that initial trespass**

gave birth to Sin, to Satan's strong influence and manipulation in our lives! And over time mankind as a whole came fully under his influence!

As a result of this new government, **as a result of this established open door, of this corruption, we all fell from the glory of God! I mean, Man was left naked and exposed! We lost our covering! We lost the glory of God! We lost our expression and exhibition of that glory**

And we were left with a distorted image of our true design! And over time we utterly lost our way, *we absolutely totally got lost!* We almost completely lost track of our true design, and our true identity as children of God, as Love's own children, *partakers of the Divine nature!*

We lost track of what it means to be made in the image and likeness of God! We lost track of what it means to actually be the image and likeness of the invisible God, *of the God who is love personified!*

You see, our whole existence now became limited to mere existence! *It became limited* **to life as a physical being in a physical environment! Even though we are more than flesh and blood *and have been so from the very beginning!***

Chapter 3

Justify Ourselves? No Way!

Genesis and Romans tells us the whole story. There in Romans 3:23 it says,

"…all have sinned and fall short of the glory of God…"

We can also look at Verse 19 there and we can clearly see that it says there that,

*"Now we know that **whatever the Law says, it speaks to those who are under the law.**"*

The Law does not just speak to those who are under the Law of Moses itself, *it does not just speak to those who are under that Law only,* but it also speaks to all those who are under the influence of the law of sin and death; under any kind of law of Man. It speaks to those who are under any kind of religious law, or moral law, or law of conscience; *even your Mother's law,* amen.

Ha… ha… ha…

He continues in Romans 3:19,

*"Now we know that **whatever the Law says, it speaks to those who are under the law. So that every mouth may be stopped and the whole world be held accountable to God;**"*

"…the whole world is accountable to God;"

"…accountable to God?"

He basically says that **the whole world *belongs to God and owes Him their existence! They owe their whole existence to Him! They owe Him their lives!* They have life because of His goodness!**

Their lives are a result of His love!

"He has richly given us all things to enjoy!"

"In Him we live and move and have our being!"

"He gives to all men, to all mankind, to all people, life, breath, and all other things!"

Why must every mouth be stopped?

Because people always *seek to justify* their lives to themselves and to others; **to so justify their lives, *outside of God!* They always seek and try to find adequate reason to justify themselves *and their life-style, even if they are a fallen creature! They try and justify their lives,* even though they have fallen away from the standard and the quality of life that God had in mind for them originally; *that God has had in mind for them from the very beginning!***

You see, we have become masters in self-righteousness! But the thing we could not escape, ***and can still not escape, is: Sin, outside of course, of the original authentic*** *truth re-revealed and redeemed in Jesus Christ* ...outside of that redemption and restoration *brought about in Him and revealed in the gospel!*

We cannot escape the power of Sin on our own!

We cannot escape the power of Sin without the work of redemption, and its truth revealed in the gospel!

Read with me Verse 9 of Romans Chapter 3,

"What then, are we Jews any better off?"

When Paul speaks of the Jews and to the Jews, he is speaking to a people, *and so he is really speaking to all people, who have the Law or any other moral and religious law **as the measuring rule for their conduct.***

He says,

"Are we any better off?"

He says,

"No, not at all!"

He says,

"For I have already made the argument and concluded my findings that both Jews and Greeks ...in fact I have come to the conclusion that all men, all people, every individual on the face of the earth ...are under the power of Sin!"

He says,

"...all men, both Jews and gentiles are under the power of Sin!"

You see, if mankind's fall *did not introduce the government of Sin then our fall would not have had all the horrible implications and consequences and results, and multiplication of sins that it did have!*

...And then Redemption could just be something like giving people merely another opportunity to exercise their choice!

But you see; mankind had to discover *that the power of our own freedom of choice is not enough to rescue us!* We had to discover that the power of our own freedom of choice **was paralyzed through that very dominion of Sin that was introduced in and through the Fall!**

Even though we can be educated in the mind to choose the right thing, **even though all kinds of moral and religious laws could be introduced, even though the Law itself could be introduced,** to instruct Man concerning good, and for Man to be educated concerning good, acceptable, moral conduct, *we soon feel ourselves paralyzed.* We soon discover and find ourselves paralyzed *under that power and that dominion of a foreign law; the law of sin and death!* We find ourselves paralyzed

by the Law behind sin and death; *the government of the Fall!*

And so the Scriptures say that,

*"...**all men, both Jew and gentile were under the power of Sin**,"*

And Paul exposes this and reveals it so clearly there in the first two chapters of Romans. He shows there how mankind, *even the person who has never known of a Law of Moses,* **felt themselves inadequate to consistently please their own conscience!**

He says that,

*"...**their own conscience would constantly accuse or at times perhaps excuse them.**"*

He shows that **there is a constant accusation against mankind** ...even against the person who is perhaps without knowledge **...**even though we as individuals may be ignorant *of the intimacy of our design and of our true relationship to God* ...**we are just left with that constant accusation against us and that ignorance. We are just left with a defiled conscience! We're left as broken people! I mean, we are just left with a God who did not leave Himself without witness; a God who did not leave Himself without evidence to His existence and His very nearness in creation,** *but whom we cannot relate to!*

Paul says that if we cannot relate to Him, *it is because* **we find within ourselves another**

Law.* And that Law restricts us from relating to Him. *It restricts us in every way! It restricts us to a defiled conscience and an accusation deep within ourselves!* <u>And therefore it consistently restricts us to symptoms of that disease in our behavior</u>. *We are restricted to symptoms of wrong behavior. That disease restricts us to behavior that does not please God; that does not please ourselves even!

Look there in Romans 3 Verse 20,

*"**For no human being will be justified in God's sight,** (or even in their own sight,) **by the works of the Law; by the law of works** (whether we try to keep Moses' Law or any other kind of religious moral or conscience law);"*

Why?

*"…**since through the Law** (through the Law of Moses or any other kind of religious moral conscience law we try to live by) **comes** (only) **the knowledge of Sin!**"*

EPEGNOSKO is the Greek word there. It's **the full knowledge** of Sin.

So, *"…**through the Law comes** (only) **the full knowledge of Sin;**"*

*The knowledge of Sin **in its full implication!***

So the law challenges us as a measuring standard **to try and measure up to that standard, to try and measure the strength** of our ability to choose what is right, what is best, to try and measure the strength of our willpower against Sin, so that we can fully measure the strength of Sin! So that we can fully discover our own total and utter weakness against it, and thus to be able to fully define the Fall and it's affects, and to therefore be able to fully define Sin! *And to at the end of this process come to the realization that we weren't designed for this inferior life!*

The law was meant to help us come to the realization that we were designed for God and that we need God! That He is indeed the fulfillment we are looking for! That His love is the only thing that can truly fulfill us! That we were not designed and therefore cannot exist, cannot live *without Him; without a genuine friendship with God!*

We cannot live without an intimate love relationship with Him!

We are meant to be His companions! Because we are indeed His offspring; *His children!*

That measuring standard of the Law *was based on His image and likeness hidden, undiscovered, within us; within the very core and make up of our being!*

Chapter 4

The Glory of God!

We can also quickly look at Galatians 3:10,

*"**Everyone who relies on the works of the Law; or on the law of works, is under a curse;**"*

They are under the curse of frustration and un-fulfillment *produced by that law of works,* as they employ that law to try and consistently obey the Law of Moses or whatever other moral or conscience law they are trying to live up to. **That curse of frustration and un-fulfillment is produced *by their self-reliance,* it is perpetuated by their *reliance upon their own efforts to try and justify themselves.***

*"...**for it is written, 'Cursed is everyone who does not abide by all the things written in the book of the Law, and do them.**"*

The problem with the Law is that it makes a demand upon a person *even though that person does not have the ability to keep the Law.*

But you see, the Law was only an indication of, and pointed to *that image and likeness hidden inside of us.*

It pointed to **God's desire to define the quality of life** He knew we would be able to live *once the power of Sin was broken.*

The Law then, in providing that standard whereby we could measure our own efforts to be justified, **revealed to us the extent of Sin's power** ...*And at the same time it awakened in us also a longing to again be restored to that innocence we once had before God before the Fall.*

Through the Law mankind now knew *that our lives would never be complete outside of innocence with God.*

We came to know that *no matter how we sought to justify ourselves in our own conduct, and how much of other people's applause we won* **through our good behavior,** *even if we won the whole community's applause,* **there still remained a large void within our spirit.**

Because if we were to be honest, every one of us knows, *deep down on the inside of us,* **that even though** *we could have reason to boast before people,* <u>we still stand there falling short of our design</u>. ...*We still stand there as a fallen creature, cut off and separated from our Maker, reduced to an inferior life to the life of our true design and identity* ...accused and condemned *in our own conscience!*

We stand there *under that cloud of condemnation* **before our Maker,** *before our Father,* **because something has happened**

to us that must be dealt with! It must be dealt with by a redemption and a justification that could only come from God! Because you see, we have fallen short of the glory of God!

Now that word *"glory"* in the Greek is the word DOXA. It's a very interesting word. It comes from the Greek word DOKAO which means: **to imagine, to form an opinion.** And the word DOXA literally means: **an opinion, or a positive reputation.**

See, when God beheld His creature, ***when God beheld us,*** **we were the expressed image of God's opinion, the expressed image of God Himself,** ***and that my friend was the very glory that clothed Man!*** We were standing there, *and we are standing there again today, thanks to Jesus ...We are standing there* **as a mirror reflection of the opinion of the God who designed us!**

So when Sin was introduced to Man and the dominion and the power of **darkness** spread through the human race, **we within ourselves lost the opinion and the approval of God! And we lost the positive reputation we had! And God could no longer approve of the creature we have become!**

God never lost track of our value!

He never lost track of your worth!

He never stopped loving you!

He never changed His mind about you!

His mind was never changed about <u>the real you</u> that is, *<u>about your original design and true identity</u>!*

<u>**God knows the real truth about you**</u>**!**

But He could not approve of the Fall and its influence upon us! *He could not approve of that deceived, inferior creature we had turned out to be because of the Fall!* **He could not approve of that deception and that corruption and that union with the Law of Sin and Death, that marriage agreement between Man and his worst nightmare, the enemy of Man and therefore also of God! He could not approve of that!**

We lost His favorable opinion and His approval! Not the real us, mind you, but the deceived and corrupted us, *this false and assumed new identity and alternative lifestyle we adopted and now lived by!*

But the real us never lost His favorable opinion and approval!

Ha... ha... ha... Hallelujah!

Thank you Papa; thank you Jesus for revealing these things to us in the incarnation and by Your Holy Spirit!

It is very essential then, in the light of these truths, to go an ponder and do a study in Scripture on that little Greek word DOXA and its true meaning, **especially in the light of the New Testament revelation that** *Jesus is the mirror image of the invisible God.* **But then**

you see, because we were also made and brought forth in God's image and likeness, Jesus is therefore not only the mirror image of the invisible God, *but He is therefore also the mirror image of the invisible us; our original design and true identity!*

Hebrews 1:2 says that,

*"**Jesus is the exact image of <u>the glory</u> of God.**"*

Thus, He was the exact reflection of the opinion of His Father! He is the exact reflection of that true and eternal opinion of His Father *concerning us, concerning the real us.* He is the exact reflection and exhibition of that opinion of His Father *concerning our original design.* He is the *true image,* the Father's exact manifested opinion about *our true identity!*

Wow! Hallelujah! Wonderful Jesus!

But let's get to Galatians 3:19 now where Paul asks this question,

*"**Of what purpose was the Law then?**"*

*"**It was added because of the transgressions;**"*

Now that word *"**added**"* in the Greek is also used for the word **to** *"**calculate.**"* In other words, *the purpose of the Law was **in order to calculate the transgressions!***

So the Law was given to Israel, *and then to the rest of mankind through Israel,* thus **the Law was given to Man as a whole, *in order for Man to be able to calculate by it.* It was given in order for Man to calculate the transgressions, in order for Man to add it all up,** *and to then come to some kind of conclusion about it!* God wanted us to come to the right conclusion, *an enlightened conclusion concerning the Fall and Sin and its fruit of sin!*

So by the Law we came *to an accurate conclusion,* ***to the right conclusion!* We came to the accurate understanding of the full extent of our Sin problem, of the full extent of our sin,** *to understand how empty it is, to understand how far it falls short from what we were originally designed for!*

The Law was given so that we could come to the conclusion that ***this is not what we were designed for!*** To conclude that this existence, **this life we now live, this alternative life-style we were reduced to because of the fall of Adam, because of the Fall,** <u>*has no glory*</u> *compared to that true glory we were custom designed for and made for to enjoy!*

So here Galatians 3 confirmed what we have seen there in Romans 3:20. Also in Romans 7:7 and in Romans 7:13 we have another reference to that same concept. But I don't want to get into that just yet. Let's rather read Romans 5 from Verse 12 right now in this light.

Chapter 5

Death; The Opposite Of ZOE!

"Therefore as Sin came into the world through one man and death through Sin;"

"...and so death spread to all men because all men sinned;"

"...death spread to all men as a result of the fact that all men partook of Sin and sinned."

Can I just quickly help you understand *"death"* in terms of the Scriptural definition? *"Death"* does not mean that we now cease to exist. We were created, *we were made,* **we were given birth to, we were brought forth, as an eternal being!**

The Greek word ZOE is the opposite of that word *"death"*. **And ZOE does not mean mere eternal existence! ZOE speaks of the life-quality that God has in mind for us!** *And so, "death" speaks of the loss of that life-quality that God has in mind for us!*

Thus, *"death"* does not mean **to cease to exist! Listen, you will exist eternally whether you like it or not,** *because you are an eternal being!*

So *"death,"* in its Scriptural and natural meaning, means: **a separation from life.** And so, in this case, in its Scriptural meaning *"death"* means: **a separation from LIFE, from the *'ZOE'* of God;** *from the very life-quality God has designed us for!*

"Death" speaks of **a separation!** It speaks of a distinct distance that has come in relationship; *in actual fellowship!* **Thus we can no longer relate to the life of God, to that 'ZOE', to that life-quality of God,** *and God can no longer relate to us! I mean, He can't relate to the new corrupted us, and we can't relate properly to God anymore; intimately! There is no more innocence there!* **There is no more agreement there! There's no common ground! We are like strangers to each other!** *We no longer find likeness in each other!*

That's what that word, *"death"* is all about. *So there is a complete disconnect and a distance relationally!* **A distinct, notable distance now exists between us and God, <u>because of the corruption that took place in the mindset of fallen Man</u>,** *and which thus corrupted his whole being!*

So when the Fall came and we *"died"* we did not cease to exist, **but in our relationship with God we ceased to exist.** I mean as far as seeing eye to eye with God is concerned, as far as us enjoying intimate relationship and fellowship with God, and as far enjoying that 'ZOE' that life-quality is concerned, we died!

That fellowship ceased to exist! *That life-quality ceased to exist!* Oh, we were still very much alive, *but we were as good as dead!*

There was now a distinct separation between us and God! And thus a distinct separation between us *and that life-quality we were designed for! We could no longer relate to the One who completes us!*

This separation was introduced *through one man's trespass!*

Through the law of identification, what that one man did *was introduced to the whole of the human race. It affected all of mankind!* The disease was passed on, it spread to all mankind, to all future generations!

Why?

Because a government was legally introduced; a disease, a virus, a parasite: *The government of **ignorance**; the government of **darkness**!*

Listen, Adam's one act of sin, his transgression, his trespass, *his fall into sin, into ignorance and confusion and darkness, became our fall.*

Why?

Because a link was established between Adam and the devil, *and Sin entered the world.* Sin was introduced and passed on to the rest of us. It spread like a parasite, like a virus or a disease! Thus the Fall was introduced to the rest of us. The Fall, that parasite, that virus, that disease, became a reality to all mankind.

The Fall represents that whole government of Sin, **that whole government of Satan!** The Fall represents everything that happened to us *as a result of the introduction of the invisible dominion of Sin,* **that invisible link established between us and <u>darkness</u>, between us and that parasite, that virus, that disease, between us and the devil and his forces of <u>darkness</u>** *that corrupts mankind.*

Do you remember when Jesus was taken up to the pinnacle of that mountain by the devil there in Luke Chapter Four? And how the devil pointed out to Him and He was shown all the glory and all the kingdoms of this world. And the devil said to Jesus that,

*"…**all these authorities were all given unto me**."*

*'**Now if You and I go into some kind of agreement on something here Jesus … some kind of partnership or something; you know, like Adam and I did, and we make some kind of contract with each other; then maybe Jesus we can share the glory of all these kingdoms, you know, just like the first Adam and I did!**'*

Satan said,

*"…**these were given to me!**"*

God never gave it to him, so where else would he have gotten it from if not through Adam?

But let's move on. So Verse 12 of Romans 5 says that,

*"**Death spread to all men since all men sinned** (or became partakers of Sin and therefore sinned);"*

Verse 13,

*"**Sin indeed was in the world <u>before</u> the Law was given, but Sin is not counted where there is no Law.**"*

And now because of misunderstanding you have people asking,

*'Then why the Law then, if the Law only came to upset the whole thing! Why did God not just leave the Law out of the equation and never introduce the Law? I mean it would have been much better that way! …**because sin wasn't counted where there was no Law**'*

Hey listen, read it correctly! He does not say that **sin didn't count!**

You see, **whether sin is counted or not,** *its effects must be dealt with!* <u>**It counts**</u>**!**

Whether you know that you've got cancer or not, <u>*you've still got the same problem*</u>! So whether we know about our sin or not, *we are still subject to the dominion of Death;* **the dominion of a life in the flesh!** We're still

subject to the dominion of that inferior life, and that inferior corrupted life-style! We're subject to a life of eking out a mere existence in the flesh! *We are subject to the dominion of death; doomed to living a mere natural life separate from God!*

So whether we knew the extent of sin in the flesh or not, *we were still subject to that Death!*

But he did not say that **sin doesn't count!**

He says that **Sin was not counted, it was not calculated, it was not added up mathematically, correctly, as to come to an accurate conclusion** *about its bondage and its misery; trapping us in an inferior life-style!* **It was trapping us in sins, trapping us in flesh-life! It was keeping us in bondage to a mere natural, inferior existence,** *and it separated us from our original design! We were disconnected from our Origin, from our Maker, from our Father, our Daddy; from the One who completes us! We were separated from that life, from that 'ZOE', that life-quality we were created to enjoy.*

And so Romans 5:14 says,

*"****Yet Death reigned from Adam to Moses.****"*

Moses is mentioned because Moses was the man through whom God introduced the Law.

So all the generations before the Law *still found mankind to be subject to death* ...Even though there was no counting during that time,

no calculation of sin *to measure the extent of Sin by!* There was nothing substantial to measure Sin against! *And Man just had to blindly accept that this is what their life was supposed to be like!*

You see, when God introduced the Law He meant for the Law to point out, ***to be some kind of reminder of the original design of Man,*** **so that Man could have a realistic measure to calculate and measure Sin against!**

Can you begin to see the nature of Man's dilemma, *of our dilemma after the introduction of the Fall?*

We no longer measured up within ourselves. We no longer measured up to the measure God has measured us by! *We didn't measure up to that measure; the life-quality He had in mind for us!* We no longer measured up to ***that glory now dormant within us!*** **We no longer measured up to that GLORY!**

Can you now see *the nature of the fall of Adam for what it was? Can you see the nature of the Fall, the nature of our dilemma?*

You see we have to see this ***so that we can appreciate the nature of our redemption!***

I hope you understand more fully now how that if Man's fall was merely Man on his own now *doing wrong things,* then Man's redemption could simply be a matter of *starting to do the right things!*

So that you see, we have all this bad conduct on the one side of the scale, and now we can just pile this good conduct on the other side of the scale, *to hopefully balance the whole thing out you know* ...**And that way, *we'll redeem Man,* and we'll work out some kind of compromised salvation!**

Listen, that could never satisfy the heart of God! **He full well knows what He has in mind for Man, *it is preserved in His opinion of Man! It is preserved within Himself; within His very own being!***

God cannot and will not be fooled!

He will not settle for less than the original *fully restored!*

He will not settle for the lie!

He won't settle for *the deception, the distortion, the corrupted version of us!*

God will not settle for what is not real!

God will only settle for the real us!

He will only settle for the original us restored* ...*the true us, our true design, our true identity* ...*redeemed* ...*restored!

Nothing less than that reality will do!

Nothing less than *His image and likeness reproduced, and fully restored,* will do!

Nothing less than that *total companionship with Man* will do!

Anything less is not a reality God will accept!

God will not settle for an alternate reality scenario!

He will not settle for any alternative to what He considers and knows to be reality!

He knows the reality of our design!

He knows our being!

He knows who you are! ...***Who you really are!***

You are His workmanship!

You are awesomely and wonderfully made!

He is your origin!

He is your Daddy!

You were put in your mother's womb ***and there you were merely clothed with flesh!***

***You are more* than flesh and blood!**

***You are a spirit-being* who merely lives in a body!**

You are God's offspring!

You are of the God-kind! ...***You are God's child!***

You are God compatible! ...*You are God's companion in life!*

You were made to share in God's LIFE, God's '*ZOE*', God's life-quality, *together with Him!*

You were made to share with Him in that same life-quality!

You were made to enjoy that specific life-quality! Nothing else, no alternative, nothing less, nothing inferior!

That is the reality about your life!

That is what God knows to be true about you!

Ha... ha... ha... Hallelujah!

Isn't that wonderful!

Isn't that just the best news ever!

Chapter 6

The Measuring Standard Of The Law!

Let's quickly go to Romans 7:7,

"What then shall we say? Shall we say that the Law is Sin? (That the Law is equal to Sin. That the Law now is also wrong; that the Law is sin!)"

"By no means!"

"If it had not been for the Law, I would not have known Sin. I would not have known that disease; what it really is to covet, if the Law has not said, 'You must not covet'"

Verse 8,

"But Sin, (that parasite, that virus, that disease,) **finding opportunity in the commandment, wrought in me all kinds of covetousness."**

"Apart from the Law, Sin lies dormant,"

It pretends to be dead, but it is quietly at work, it is operating still, but in stealth mode, without showing itself for what it really is, **until it gets challenged.** Then it (becomes activated,) its true self, *its power* is revealed. This Sin is that invisible prince of the power of the air: Satan himself!

It is interesting to note that the name, Satan or Devil comes for the old Hebrew language and was adopted into the Greek language. In the Greek the word is: SATANAS, which means: **an adversary, one who resists,** and the word DIABOLOS, which means: **slanderous, accusing or accusation.** It goes right along with the word, Sin, which means: **to miss the mark, or to miss the point.** That word, sin, is the word, HAMARTIA in the Greek, which means: **that which has no value, or is of no merit.** It also goes right along with the word: evil, as in *the tree of the knowledge of good and **evil**.* That word, **evil** in the Greek is the word, PANEROS which means: **Hardship, labors, toil and frustration.**

But let's get back to Romans 7:9,

*"**I was once alive apart from the Law,** (or so I thought) **but when the commandment came, Sin revived and I died!**"*

No let's face it, if you read that, you could get confused and wonder, *what in the world is Paul saying here?* Is he saying that introducing the Law was a big mistake? Is he saying that the Law should never have been introduced? Is he saying that the Law is bad; that *it is the cause of sin?* ...that the Law *brought sin into the world; that it established the government of Sin?* Is that what he is saying?

*'I mean, Paul, what are you saying man? Listen Paul, **the Law is holy and righteous and just and good!** I mean, **the Law represents everything good! There is nothing offensive in the Law! The Law represents that which is good!** So, please explain yourself Paul! And make sure you don't get confused yourself! Make things clear man, don't confuse us now brother Paul, with statements like; "**I was once alive apart from the Law!**" But then you say, 'The Law came in and actually just upset the whole balance of things.' I mean, as you say, "**I was once alive!**"*

Listen have you read Ephesians 2:1–5 lately?

It says, *"**We who were dead, in our trespasses, in which we lived…**"*

It says, *"**We were alive, never the less we were dead!**"*

It says, *"**You were dead, never the less you lived, yet not you, but Sin lived within you!**"*

I mean **what kind of life is that?**

And so Verse 13 of Romans 7 says,

*"**Did that which is good then, bring death to me?**"*

Paul says,

*"**By no means!** It was Sin, working death in me, through what is good **in order that Sin might be shown to be sin indeed, and**†*

through the commandment might become sinful ...<u>beyond measure</u>!"

In other words: ...**<u>totally intolerable</u>**!

"*...so that* **through the commandment Sin and sin might become <u>totally intolerable</u>**"

Now I remind you of the subject of this book. We are looking at and studying: *"The measure of a Man,"* or more accurately, **the measure God has measured the human being by; the measure God measures us by** ...**the measure God has measured you by!**

In my book: *No Longer Looking for Applause,* we looked at and studied mankind's alternative measure for righteousness. We studied Humanity's standard of wisdom, and Society's standard of what is called noble birth; the World's standard of what they call strength and skill and achievement, *and how God had to come in and expose the deception, and the hypocrisy of our standards!*

And He did it through the Law! Because the Law had to come and highlight sin, in order to introduce Sin for its true colors, *so that Sin could be shown to be sin* (or totally intolerable) **beyond measure!**

That means that the Law came in as a measure!

…And the measure of the Law would seek to **confine sin**; and thus **define Sin!**

The measure of the Law would seek to confine our behavior within a certain limit! And it would say to us, *'Don't break through that boundary. You should keep your conduct within this boundary.' This is what is good, not that!* And in doing so, *sin was challenged,* ***and thus Sin was challenged!***

Listen, we had to discover that there was more to the Fall of Man than just some kind of blunder, just some kind of trip-up, some kind of mistake that Adam and Eve made ...*something that just kind of **temporarily** tripped them up, some kind of **temporary**, abnormal **anomaly** they encountered there in the Garden.*

We had to all discover that we were made subject to some kind of dominion that had to be broken!

We had to discover that even our own dust, our own flesh bodies, and our own fleshly desires, even our destructive lusts *were merely the symptoms and not the real problem!*

Because you see, *there was an invisible power that exploited us and brought about the Fall of Man and kept us bound and captive to our own desires and destructive lusts!*

And so the Law came and introduced **a measure** *that would challenge the measure of Man's own ability,* **the measure of our own** *strength; the measure of our own ability to discipline our conduct.*

The Law came and introduced that measure *that would be measure enough to challenge the measure of our own ability,* **and so to show our sins to be sin** *...to be intolerable, beyond measure!*

The Law came to reveal sin to merely be the fruit of Sin; it thus came to reveal Sin to be Sin; *intolerable beyond measure!* **...*Out of all proportions!* ...*And outside of our control!* ...*And outside of what we were designed for!* ...*Totally outside of what we can handle or bear!***

I mean it is poison to us! It releases toxic, destructive forces! It produces death! It is dangerous, toxic, destructive, wrong, and evil! *It causes us to live life in self-destruct-mode!* **And it means only one thing: the perpetuation of spiritual death;** *of Death itself!* **It is totally totally beyond measure, out of bounds, and intolerable;** *unacceptable, toxic and detrimental in every way!*

The Law came to show sin to be sin beyond measure! And thus it also came to show Sin to be sin beyond measure!

It's like trying to keep a wild animal caged in! **But every day that animal breaks through that fence,** and so you decide, '*I'm going to build the fence stronger and higher!*'

...And that is exactly what society has tried to do through legislation. They have tried to so fence people's conduct *into the pattern, into the measure of what we as a society approves of, and of what the whole civilized world would approve of,* **that they have introduced law after law after law.**

Listen man, you can go and study the history of the Jews, how they have introduced, above the Ten Commandments, *hundreds of other commandments,* **hundreds of little things, nit-picky little things,** *which is supposed to try and regulate people's conduct and force them into good behavior,* **and you will see how the Law failed.**

Why?

Because it just couldn't change the effects of the Fall! It couldn't change Sin's distorted nature! *It couldn't undo that lie, that deception, that corruption that ruled in Man!* **It could not undo that Sin:** *That ruling mentality, that ruling mindset,* **that ruling bent towards sin,** *that ruling lie and deception, that foreign ruling force, that parasite, that virus, that disease within Man.*

Sin and it's fruit of sin; that lie and deception, that ruling mentality and mindset, and its corruption in the lives of people *proved to be too strong to be broken* **by mere choices and willpower!**

Listen; you cannot change the nature of a parasite!

No. You can only free a person from that parasite, and then that person will return to their own normal state of being; their normal state of health.

You see, **religion is always busy treating symptoms,** *and yet never dealing with the disease itself!*

You can curb the conduct of any creature *through regular discipline and reward,* and you can even turn a wild animal into a circus animal *and get it to behave just right.* **But until you release it back *into its natural environment, its true design,* all your efforts to change its misbehaving will prove to be ineffective! You will fail!**

Listen, we weren't designed for the cage of Sin!

And neither were we designed for the cage of religion, nor the cage of legalism!

...but you see, trying to turn us all into circus animals, that is exactly what religion and society has tried to do, instead of introducing Mankind to the truth, to the true gospel, which is the power of God.

They have tried to turn us all into docile, obedient, performing circus animals, instead of introducing real change, by removing that force that leads to the corruption of Man's nature, by removing that *corruption and that distortion out of our being; <u>introducing us back to our original design,</u>* and introducing to us *<u>our true identity</u>.*

Instead of introducing that real change *through introducing real truth; the truth of God, the truth of the gospel,* they have merely introduced to Man rules and regulations that would endeavor to curb his conduct, *and yet leave his nature unchanged, unaffected by their efforts, and <u>still corrupted</u>!*

Now what is the result of all that? **Utter failure!**

...**Even under religion** ...*especially under religion!*

I dare say: All the religions of Man have failed us, bar none; *including the Christian religion!* ...*and because of religion, mankind has continued to live under condemnation, trapped in sin-consciousness* ...and therefore even greater condemnation and frustration and un-fulfillment, and failure!

That is exactly why today still most of humanity continues to live *void of the glory of God* ...*void of intimacy with God* ...**even though Christ has come, and redemption is a reality!**

You see, even though the true gospel has been introduced and God's ultimate truth has been revealed, most of humanity still continue to live void of the glory of God! ...They live void of intimacy with God.

Ignorance is to blame for that!

A darkened understanding is to blame for that!

Man-made religion is to blame for that!

But God could not and cannot accept that as any alternative to His plan!

So He came in person, in the incarnation, to fix it!

I have good news for you! Jesus did not come to start yet another religion, to, you know, compete with all the other religions of this world! Jesus did not come to start the Christian religion; we did that, all on our own, in our ignorance ...in His name maybe, but not representing accurately what He truly promotes! Jesus did not come to confirm any of our religions; or to establish His own, no, *He simply came as an open statement of the truth! He came to represent that which was true in God and in us from the very beginning. He came to show us the Father, and He came to show us who we really are as children of God. He came to put the image and likeness of God on display.* He came to unveil the invisible spectacular God! He said: *"If you've seen Me, you've seen the Father!"* But not only that, He was both the Son of God and the son of Man. *Jesus came to reveal us, the real us, to us! He came in person; God came in person to reveal himself and to reveal His love for us to us! He came to reveal to us who we really are as children of God; and He came to reveal to us our value to Him, our true worth to Him! He came to reveal that He is Mr. LOVE personified and that we are worth everything to Him! He came to show us that He always has been, and still is, in love with us!* Jesus came, and even though we rejected Him, he laid down His life in His overwhelming love for us, *to prove that love to us; to convince us of our value and worth to Him* ...*and He thereby stripped Satan of his authority; He thus also destroyed Sin's power, all in one event, in one act, in one glorious display of His love for us! He introduced and unveiled the light and shattered our ignorance and our darkness! Darkness was utterly defeated in Him!*

I want you to see very clearly that through His death on that cross, *through such a clear display of His love for us,* He released us fully of the very thing that had us bound, *and He thus condemned Sin in the flesh; He released us from its strong grip; its strangle-hold.*

He set us free!

He made us whole again!

Redemption is now a reality!

The restoration of all things has already come!

God has successfully done it in Christ!

Ha... ha... ha... Hallelujah!

Oh the tremendous, magnificent, mysterious power of **God's love revealed!**

There is enough power in the grace of God, *in the display of the love of God for us,* to set the whole of mankind, every single one of us, free!

He came to set us free from sin, not free to sin!

He came to set us free from the power of Sin itself!

He came to us free to be free indeed!

He came to set us free to know and believe we are loved!

He came to set us free in love, for love, to enjoy His love, and be love ourselves!

He came to make us whole!

But people still keep being confused about the cross of Christ and about the work of redemption.

Why? **Because of religion! Because of man-made ideas! Because of cleverly devised little myths and fables and theories and philosophies *born out of sheer*** *ignorance and guesswork,* **and now being sold to a confused humanity as some kind of cure to their problem!**

Every religion has its own message, its own gospel! But as I said before, I thank God that Jesus didn't come to start a religion! He didn't even come to start the Christian religion! ***True Christianity is not a religion!*** **Christianity is a real, genuine relationship with Jesus Christ and with Father God in the Spirit!**

Listen, God wants nothing to do with fake religion! He wants nothing to do with religion, period!

He is only interested in relationship, *a true intimate relationship with <u>you</u>!*

I say again: **Jesus came as an open statement of God's eternal truth, of God's truth about Himself,** *that He is LOVE! He came as an open statement of God's truth about us, about our true identity and design!* **He came to introduce the gospel of God! He came with real good news! He came to reveal and redeem God's true image and likeness! He came to reveal and redeem the image and likeness of God inside of fallen Man! He came to restore our original design and true identity as children of God! He came to awaken and release the image and likeness of God in us! He came to set us free to be our authentic selves! Our original selves! He**

came to free us and release us! He came with that message!

It is good news! It is the real thing! The true gospel!

As I said, *even the Christian religion still doesn't get the true gospel!* Neither does any other religion! Religion doesn't preach that message **because it doesn't know that message!**

The mystery of God has been revealed *but they still continue to live in a mystery!*

The riddle of life has been solved! *But they still don't know it!*

Because of that, *religion only ever perpetuates its own blindness!*

Sincere, well-meaning religious people ***are still confused themselves,*** and therefore, in spite of all their efforts, **they only perpetuate blindness! I mean, *they still keep obscuring the truth for the rest of mankind, because it is obscure to them!***

But I thank God that Jesus said,

*"****You shall <u>know</u> the truth and the truth shall make you free!****"*

Listen, there is no excuse for our ignorance! *Not anymore!*

Life's riddle *has been solved!*

There is no excuse for the Church of the Lord Jesus Christ *to remain ignorant* **or to remain confused!**

*...*And therefore there is no more excuse for us *to keep the rest of the world ignorant and confused either!*

The world is only ignorant and confused *because of us!* **Because we are not doing our job! Because we don't make it our aim to show ourselves approved, a worker that does not need to be ashamed,** *rightly dividing the word of truth!*

*...*Because we do not take the time as Christians, morning by morning, <u>daily</u>, *to have our ears awakened to the real gospel, to the accurate truth of God, so that we may have the tongue <u>of the learned</u>,* like the pen of a ready writer, so that we <u>may be able</u> to rescue the rest of God's kids, *by engraving His love upon their inner-being, impacting them with the truth of His love; awakening their hearts to His genuine love for them.*

I cannot stress enough that *we need to have the impact of the gospel engraved upon our own hearts first. We need to gain a thorough understanding of the truth revealed in the gospel, for ourselves, I mean that message is for us, the gospel speaks to us first, impacting our hearts with His love for us, and also for the whole world, for all His other kids as well* ...So that we then may be able to rescue the world <u>with the Word of truth</u>, with the gospel, the good news of our salvation, and their salvation, *already accomplished in Christ!*

Rightly Isaiah said some terrible things concerning us, **concerning our ignorance.**

Isaiah 42:19,

*"**Who is as dumb as My servants?**"*

Ha… ha… ha…

No! Relax Max! I'm not one of those beat-you-up preachers!

Ha… ha… ha…

He actually said in Verse 18,

"**Hear, you deaf** …**And look, you blind, <u>that you may see</u>**."

In Verse 19, He starts talking about Christ, *His measure by which He measured,*

"**Who is blind but My Servant?**"

"**Or as deaf as My Messenger whom I send?**"

"**Who is as blind as the Lord's Servant?**"

Verse 20,

"**Seeing many things** …**but you do not observe**;"

"**Opening the ears** (saying many things) … **but He does not hear.**"

Listen, read that scripture *very carefully* again, in its context, *and you will see how it prophetically points to Jesus* **walking in love, refusing to judge anyone, *seeing them through the eyes of the Father, and refusing to see them any other way*.**

He did not entertain a negative report concerning Man, *not even concerning the Pharisees!*

No. He loved them all and refused to enter into accusation. He refused to entertain the voice of the Accuser; of Satan!

God wants to give us a new measure to measure ourselves and the rest of mankind by! He wants to give us the measure of His Servant; *the measure of Christ!*

He wants to give us the same measure Christ saw us by and measured us all by! The same light He saw us in! *The light of original truth! The light of our original design! The light of our Daddy's love!*

Jesus saw us all *in the light of redemption! The redemption of our original design and true identity!* He saw us *in that* light! That was His *only* measure!

Ha... ha... ha... Hallelujah!

Chapter 7

The Nature Of Sin!

Let's continue on so that we may gain some more revelation together; *some more insight and understanding.* Don't you appreciate the flow of the Holy Spirit?

Teach us Lord! **Open our eyes some more!**

So, *"**Sin was shown to be sin beyond measure!**"*

No measure of Man's legislation and of Man's good year's resolutions, **no measure of good resolutions, not even under religion, can consistently affect and curb Man's behavior, in the hope of sufficiently changing his conduct!** Humanity so easily becomes captive and falls prey *to their own ability to work and perform!* The hustle and bustle of our over developed modern society has proven that! Religion has proven that!

But I thank God that,

*"**The path of the just** (of the redeemed), **is like the light of dawn, it grows brighter and brighter until the Son,** (not the sun, but the Son) **establishes day**..."*

Ha... ha... ha...

And if you walk in the footsteps of righteousness with your Shepherd, David says,

"Surely goodness and mercy shall follow me all the days of my life!"

Hallelujah! **What guarantee can you compare with that!**

So, *"Sin was shown to be sin beyond measure!"* **So that man could discover the need to return, the need for a redemption, a redemption** *that would be much larger than his own effort, than his own ability to try and perform and improve himself* **...or to perform so correctly, that eventually he would please God and find God's approval and be restored in God's measure!**

We might as well, while we are in Romans 7, look at Verse 14 also.

"We know that the Law is spiritual, but I am carnal, sold under Sin!"

Many religious teachers, educated even, sincere theologians, many educated and sincere scholars, *but sincerely wrong,* have thought that Paul was here in Romans 7 just writing about his own experience *as a Christian.* In fact, one of my Bibles even has it as a heading there: *"The Christian's Struggle".*

No man. It would have been more appropriate to say: *"The Theologian's Struggle".*

Ha… ha… ha…

How can Paul be speaking about himself as being, *"...**sold under Sin**" ...as a Christian?* Especially when in Chapter Six, Verse 6 of that same letter to the Romans, he writes and says,

"We know that our old selves were crucified with Him** ...so that the **Sinful Body** (that union between me and Sin) might be destroyed ...and we might no longer be enslaved to Sin (and therefore to sins)!"

How could we possibly be speaking of the same person here? One has already been *released from the slavery of sin,* and yet you have the same person supposedly also saying, *'Here I am, the real me now, not the front I'm trying to put up in front of others, and O, if I'm going to have to be really honest here, I have to admit, **I'm still a slave of sin.'***

Listen, that was not the same person speaking about his new life in Christ! **That was not Paul's testimony as a Christian!** Who is Paul speaking to in Romans 7? Let's look at Verse 1 of Chapter 7.

He says, ***"Do you not know brethren, for I am** (now) **speaking to those who <u>know</u> the Law** (...who live by and under the Law)!"*

Paul is addressing those who know the Law and in their knowledge of the Law *have sought all their lives long to be justified through the Law.* He says to them, *'I am very familiar with your life under the Law, remember, I lived it too, but let's be real honest now, about our life and our efforts under the Law...'* I mean, we can easily go and look at Paul's own experience in these matters, we can go look at Paul's pedigree and qualifications in Judaism and in the Law, *there in Philippians 3.*

He said, Verse 4,

*"****Look, if I had reason to boast**** ...****If any man has any reason to boast in the flesh****,"* he says, *"****I've had more reason than they!****"*

And he proceeded to tell us there in verse 5 and 6 all about his past and his pedigree and every positive thing he could possibly name, and how according to the Law even, *in front of people,* he lived a blameless life! **...But not in private; not within himself** ...because now here in Romans 7, he gets real honest about that life under the Law, and he points out and he says about that life he used to live, (speaking to those who are under the Law, as if he was still living under the Law himself), he says, *"****I do not understand my own actions,*** *that is, my actions under the Law"*

Look at this in Verse 15 of Romans 7, Paul is still describing the struggle he had under the Law,

*"****For I do not do what I want, but I do the very thing that I hate. Now, if I do what I do not want, I agree that the Law is good!****"*

Paul says in other words that,

*'****I have already been instructed through the Law, and in my heart I agree that the Law is good. I really don't, in my heart, feel that***

the Law is asking too much of me! ...And that the Law is wrong and bad and that we better change the Law or do away with the Law ...and ban that sucker!'

Ha... ha... ha...

Paul says,

'No man, I have an agreement in my heart, deep inside of me, which bears witness with the goodness of the Law. I'm in agreement with the Law, with that goodness in the Law. I know that that Law provides me with a good standard ...which if I try and follow that good standard, it becomes a standard of possible innocence before God!'

He says,

'<u>The real me</u>, I'm in agreement!'

But now he says,

'Even if I'm in agreement with the Law, there is something else also going on here. I'm beginning to notice some other force at work here as well! Some other force, contrary to me, <u>to the real me, to my real design</u>, working within me, manipulating me, controlling me! ..."For I do not do what I want, but I do the very thing that I hate"

He says,

'I agree with the goodness I see in the Law, <u>but</u> "now if I do what I do not want," then

whether I agree with the goodness of the Law or not, I also must see the power of Sin! …and then I must agree also that Sin is at work in my life!'

Remember now, he is still speaking to those who intimately know the Law and its whole system; *to those who have lived under that system and have sought all their lives long to be justified through the Law*.

And this now is the interesting thing about Paul's findings while living under the Law, Paul discovered that,

'***If I then do what I do not want, then this is the logical conclusion;***'

Look at verse 17,

"***So then, it is no longer I that do it, but Sin which indwells me.***"

Do you see the conclusion the Law brings us to? And not just the Law, *any kind of religious law that addresses our conduct,* **even Islamic law, or Hinduism, or Buddhism, or Mormonism, or whatever other religious law or rule of conscience and conduct we are trying to live by.**

I mean, not just the Law of Moses, **any kind of moral or spiritual law or conscience law we try to apply to our conduct and try to live by, <u>it speaks to us</u>! ...And it inevitably leads us to that same conclusion Paul came to, if we would only be honest enough with ourselves to care to hear <u>that conclusion</u>**

beyond what we are engaged in at face value; beyond even our religion itself!

Listen, I am not saying now that all beliefs are equal and that we are just on different paths up the mountain, but on opposite sides of the same mountain, *and all that philosophical nonsense eastern religions try to sell us!*

Listen, just because you believe something wholeheartedly doesn't make it the truth.

The faith of Man, or man-made beliefs, doesn't equal the faith of God, or God's belief! ...And the faith of God, God's belief, God's truth became manifest and was revealed in the incarnation; in the person of Jesus Christ. He was truth personified. He said, John 14:9, *"If you've seen Me, you've seen the Father!"* **He was the exact representation of the invisible God, and therefore He is the ALPHA and OMEGA, the author and finisher of faith;** *faith is defined in Him!* - Colossians 1:15 & Hebrews 12:2

You see, **every religion of this world,** *bar none,* **is just fallen Man's best effort to discover themselves,** *or to discover a God whom they cannot see and cannot know on their own.* **I mean, the very definition of religion is fallen Man's efforts to try and figure out** *what Man is like, and what God is like,* **and to try and figure out what God wants,** *and then to try and please Him! The only problem is that God lives in the unseen realm of reality! He cannot be seen,* *and He cannot be known, <u>unless He reveals Himself</u>!*

...<u>And He did that in only one event, the incarnation, and in only one person, the person of Jesus Christ</u>!

The FULLNESS of the Godhead dwelt in Him in bodily form, and the LOGOS, the very logic of God became flesh in Jesus! - Colossians 2:9

John 1:18, *"**No one has at any time seen God or known God. But, the Son <u>who is in the bosom of</u>** (who is intimately acquainted with) *the Father, He has revealed and declared Him!"*

Let me repeat what I said earlier, so it sinks in. Jesus said, *"**If you've seen Me, <u>you've seen the Father!</u>**"* - John 14:9

Religion gave it their sincerest effort, *their best guess,* **they are very sincere,** *but they have all missed it. They are all equally wrong!*

That's why God had to come and reveal Himself! *Because they all missed it!*

Their conclusions fall short! They fall short of the glory of God!

Therefore, the Law may have been given through Moses, ***BUT THEN grace and truth came in Jesus Christ!***

Religion is religion, *and has nothing to do with the truth!*

All truths, I mean **all faiths** *cannot be equal, and <u>aren't</u> equal!*

Either it is the truth you are busy with, *or it is a lie; a half-truth at best!*

...So let me put it as plain as I possibly can: **If we are not busy with God's truth, with God's faith,** *which He himself brought into the world when He came in person and took on flesh and blood and became a man, in the person of Jesus Christ,* **<u>then we are not busy with truth or faith at all</u>!**

Whatever is not the truth *as God sees it, and as God knows it, and as God has revealed it in the original blueprint Son, in the man, Jesus Christ,* **is nothing but lies and deception and confusion;** *a wrong conclusion* ...**or at best a half-truth,** *or a miss-understanding of truth!*

God came and revealed Himself in Jesus Christ! He did not come to compete with religion. **Jesus did not come to** *compete over truth* **with Moses or Muhammad, or Buddha or whomever! He is the truth! He is truth** *personified!* **Truth is a person. His name is Jesus Christ!**

Confucius, Moses, Muhammad, Buddha and the rest *were all looking for the truth,* **but whatever little bit of truth they found,** *if any,* **is only true** *because it agrees with the truth of God revealed in Jesus Christ.*

Truth comes from God.

We do not define truth.

God defines truth!

<u>***And God has defined truth for us, and revealed truth for us, in one person; the person of Jesus Christ***</u>*!*

Paul says in Romans 2 that Man is without excuse before God **when it comes to knowing truth,** *"…because whatever can be known of God is already revealed within them!"*

That truth that is revealed only points to the nature of God, to His image and likeness, *and therefore it points to our original design.*

The truth of God which He reveals has to do with His image and likeness *in us!* **Nothing more,** *nothing less!*

That is the ultimate truth God wants us to discover and know!

That truth was obscured and hidden for ages and generations, *hidden in God* **and buried in us** *if you will,* ready to be revealed in the last days, **and then resurrected** *"in the fullness of time,"* Paul says, *in Christ, in His work of redemption!*

I want you to know that *the fullness of time came!* **Paul says** *it already came!* **That truth of God came in person. Truth is a person. His name is Jesus Christ!**

God came in person, in Jesus Christ, *and revealed Himself;* His image, His likeness, His nature! And therefore He revealed <u>us</u> to us! *Our original, authentic design!*

He came to reveal what it means to be the image and likeness of God in a man!

He came to reveal that original life-quality we were designed for to be and enjoy between us and God!

Truth became flesh and dwelt among us, *and it was revealed to be within us!*

And we beheld that glory; *His beauty!* We beheld the glory of our original design *on display in Him!* We beheld His <u>*glory*</u>! And we beheld our <u>*glory*</u> also! The very glory we lost is the glory He has come to restore to us! It was the accurate opinion of God *concerning us! His love for us was on display!* His approval of us, of our design, His approval and applause of our being, of us, of our true design and identity, *His favor towards us as His kids, was on display in Jesus Christ ...even while we rejected Him and nailed Him to a cross!*

Jesus said,

"I am the way, the truth, and the life! And no one comes back to the Father, except through Me ...through My work of redemption ...through embracing My work of redemption ...through embracing that truth ...through embracing God's love and

embracing their glorification in Me ... through embracing that glory ...embracing that glory again ...embracing that LIFE ... embracing the life of it ...embracing that life-quality again ...embracing the DOXA, that DOKAO of God!"

We've got to embrace the love and favor and truth of God revealed in Jesus! Only the truth can rescue us from the lies we have invented, believed and lived! There is no other rescue, no other remedy to the Fall of Man! There is no other option! The alternative is no option at all! To continue to live our lives in self-destruct mode is no real option at all!

I mean, why continue in a lie when the truth has so clearly been revealed! Self-deception leads to nothing but self-destruction!

What I am trying to do is to get you to see the conclusion the law brings us to. And not just the Law of Moses, the Law of God, *but any kind of religious law or moral code that addresses our conduct,* even Islamic law, or Hinduism or Buddhism or Mormonism *or whatever other religious law or rule of conscience and conduct people are trying to apply to their conduct and trying their best to live by.* ***It all speaks to us!***

And it inevitably leads us to that same conclusion the Law of Moses was sent to bring us to! If we would only care to hear

that conclusion beyond even our own choice of religion we are engaged in at face value!

Whether it is Judaism, the Christian Religion, Hinduism, Buddhism, *or whatever other religion,* **whatever moral code or code of conscience and conduct we are involved in** *...even if you do not follow any religion* **but still trying to follow your conscience, being a Humanist or a Progressive and a person that is against religion** ...**if you are at all trying to live by the golden rule** ...**or perhaps the politically correct mindset of the part of society you associate with** ...*or even if you are just trying to be yourself and just be a good person on your own,* **you still have a conscience trying to lead you to the same conclusion.**

Listen you Christians, don't get all bent out of shape now *and think that I am sponsoring and promoting Humanism or Progressive thinking now, or any other religion either,* **other than the true Christian faith!** Don't think I am saying that it's a good thing, *and that there is any kind of truth in it* or that it's okay to be involved in Humanism or Progressive Liberalism, or Conservatism, or Islam and Hinduism and Buddhism and Mormonism *and whatever other political or religious belief you can think of.* **I am not promoting any of that!**

All I am saying *is that* **every person** *on the face of this planet* **has a witness inside of them by the Spirit of God.** They have a spirit-witness <u>within their spirits and within their conscience,</u> *<u>within the very consciousness of their being, which bears witness to the existence of, and nearness and presence of God, and to the truth of their original design and their true identity,</u>* <u>whether they care to agree with me or not</u>!

But I am not saying that that voice within them, that spirit-witness *bears witness to their religion or to their political beliefs or any other beliefs they hold dear to!*

The Spirit of God <u>bears witness with their spirit</u> *<u>to the truth of their original design.</u>*

He bears witness within our spirit *that we are indeed the offspring of God.*

He does not bear witness to politics or religion ...not even the Christian religion!

The voice of religion and politics in your head, and *the voice of truth that resonates in your spirit,* is not the same thing!

Your spirit knows God's truth!

It' knows that truth of your original design, which speaks louder than any other voice, *louder than any other religious voice or political and societal belief-system and way of thinking!*

And therefore, when the truth of the gospel comes to you, *it bears witness with your spirit; it resonates within you, and confirms that truth deep within your being, which your heart already knows to be true.*

You see, **you were custom designed for God's truth! And your spirit recognizes that truth when it hears it,** *even if your mind disagrees with it; even if it violates your whole belief-system! ...Even if it is contrary to anything you have ever known or believed to be truth, or have been taught to be truth in religion and society, no matter even what religion or society you have grown up in, or have been involved in, Christian or otherwise!*

God's truth is bigger than religion!

God's truth is bigger than politics!

God's truth is bigger than society's beliefs!

God's truth is bigger than your beliefs!

Your spirit recognizes God's truth. **If you would just listen to your heart, <u>not just your head</u>,** *your heart will confirm it!*

"Faith comes by the hearing of the word!"

That means, when the truth of the gospel comes to you, *faith comes to you!*

Ha... ha... ha...

So, you literally have to reject the faith that comes to you; you have to consciously reject the faith that is being imparted to you and awakened in you by the gospel, *by the accurate communication and impartation of*

the truth of the gospel, in order to not be influenced and challenged by it!

In other words, **your heart bears witness to that truth and when you understand it with your heart, when you intelligently grasp it and comprehend it with you heart, as well as your head, *you consciously have to violate your own conscience in order to reject it!***

Ha... ha... ha... What a mouth full!

Now, keep your finger or a bookmark there in Romans 7, we'll get back to it. But I want us to go and take a look quickly at Ephesians 2. I want to point out something very significant there. A lot of the so called *"Christian"* doctrines and teachings that are out there today have kept the believers in bondage *by holding us responsible for our own sin!*

If you are a Christian, then most likely you have been taught, *'Listen, brother, listen sister,* ***just pray this sinner's prayer; just choose Jesus*** *…salvation is just a choice* **to <u>follow</u> Jesus!'**

They have tried to say to you, *'Listen, brother, listen sister,* ***sin is just a choice!****'* They have tried to tell you, *'Sin is a choice! You can choose to sin, and you can simply choose not to sin. Sin is just a choice!'*

But listen to me now: **If sin were a mere choice,** then brother, then sister, ***your whole redemption would also just be a mere*** *matter of <u>choice</u>! ...And I can simply <u>choose</u> not to sin anymore!*

But you see, my question is: **Then why preach the gospel? Then what's the need for Jesus? Why did the truth have to be revealed in Jesus? Then why do we need to understand these things. Why is it so important? And then, what is the purpose of His death? Why did Jesus come and <u>die</u>? I mean, then Jesus' death means nothing! I mean, then Jesus didn't need to face such a brutal death on a cross and the resurrection would carry no further significance!**

Yet Paul makes it plain that, *"If Christ was not raised from the dead, we would yet be in our sins!"* - 1 Corinthians 15:17

Galatians 2:21 also says this:

"If righteousness comes through the Law (through my own willpower to obey the Law; through my own choices,) *then Christ died in vain!"*

And Ephesians 2 talks about <u>the fact</u> that we **were actually ruled by the power of Sin** *and that Sin was powerful beyond measure* ...**and only in redemption,** *only in Christ,* **only in the renewing of the mind,** *through the power of the gospel;* **only through that faith being imparted and awakened,** *through revelation knowledge, only through insight and understanding, and only through the LIFE that comes with it being*

***imparted to our spirits by that Spirit of Truth, the Spirit of God,* <u>can we be truly set free</u>!**

I also want to point out to you that in Ephesians 2:2 Paul talks about that **power of Sin** that once ruled us, and about the life we once lived, he says, *"…**in which you once walked, following the course of this world**…"*

Actually let's start in verse one. And I'm reading to you from the Ruach Translation now.

Ephesians 2:1,

*"**When you were still dead towards God, you were alive in your trespasses and your sins** …**according to the course of this world. You were under the dominion of an invisible authority. This spirit ruler is even now at work in the lives of those who disregard the gospel**."*

Galatians 2:20 confirms that. It says,

*"**You were dead, nevertheless you lived, yet not you but Sin lived within you.**"*

Verse 3 of Ephesians 2 says,

*"**We were all once in his grip** (in the devil's grip) ***through the lusts of our flesh*** **(dominated by the senses, by external senses and stimulants)**.*"

*"**His strategy was to rule us through the desires of body and mind.**"*

"And we, like the rest of the human race, were, by that influence, that corruption, that distortion of our design, children of impulse."

Now let's read it from the RSV also.

Ephesians 2:1-3,

"And you He made alive even when you were dead through the trespasses and sins"

"…in which you <u>once</u> walk<u>ed</u>;"

"…following the course of this world;"

"…following the prince of the power of the air;"

"…the spirit that is even now still at work in the sons of disobedience."

He says,

"…following the course of this world;"

Now, often we would seek to justify our conduct, by saying,

'Well, everybody is doing it!'

Have you heard that before?

Ha… ha… ha…

So the course of this world would be our justification! **We would silence our conscience and say to ourselves, *'I'll get away with this kind of conduct, because, after all, it's the course of this world!'***

So here's a nice excuse, a nice solution for our problem: **Let's blame it on the world!** Let's blame it on **the modern age!** Let's blame it on **our society,** on our **Progressive thinking! I mean, *we are not that old fashioned as to believe the things taught in the Bible anymore!***

Paul says,

*"**We were following the course of this world.**"*

But there is another thing we were *following!*

*"**We were following the prince of the power of the air!**"*

You can call it *the invisible dominion.*

Paul says,

*"**We were following the spirit that now works; that spirit that is even now still at work in the sons of disobedience**"*

In verse 3 he says,

*"**Among these we all <u>once</u> liv<u>ed</u> in the passions of our flesh.**"*

He says,

*"**We were following the desires of body and mind!**"*

*"…**and so we were by nature,**"*

He says,

*"**We were the children** (the products) **of a twisted mind!**"*

Did you know that Sin has a nature? It has its own nature! *It wasn't just me following my own desires!*

You see, if it was just me, then brother, I will have to so change and educate myself with some kind of books, or courses, which contains some kind of self-help subject ...and this psychology class, and that philosophy ...maybe some eastern Buddhism or Zen thinking, and this, that, and the other thing, and use all that knowledge, and tell myself that I'm just going to have to change my conduct, and so discipline myself *that eventually I will get out of this wrong conduct!*

But listen, Paul makes it clear here that there were three other things involved here!

1. **The course of this world**
2. **That invisible dominion**
3. **The influence of that foreign, invisible nature upon my thinking and my body and my conduct and my very being!**

He talks about following the course of this world, just following along like everyone else, justifying myself, thinking, *'...too many other people experiencing the very same struggle I've been experiencing!'*

But what was the real problem?

The dominion of an invisible power!

So, if we want to look at redemption we need to begin there! **We need to discover that what God did in Christ Jesus *stripped the devil of his invisible power to rule Man and exhibit his nature in Man, independent of Man's co-operation!***

Listen, Satan no longer has any power over your life *independent of your co-operation*!

I want you to clearly see it! I want you to be *so totally persuaded about it,* before you are even done with this book!

Chapter 8

The Power Of Sin Must Be Broken!

So let's quickly go back to Romans 7. This was before Christ came. The Law could instruct me concerning that which is good, *but I find within me such conflict,* because I know that the Law is good, I want to do it, it is the very thing I want to do, I desire to do, **but it's the thing I fail to do!**

Why?

Because of another dominion that is not yet broken!

And so now, let's look at that dominion!

Romans 7:17 says,

"So then, it is no longer I that do it, but Sin which indwells me."

Do you now see that salvation must be more *than just outwardly changing my behavior?* **It must be more than trying to wipe away one cobweb at a time, no, *the spider must be removed!* The power of sin and its indwelling influence upon me must be broken!**

And that's exactly what Jesus Christ _did_! That's exactly what our faith takes a hold of! That's the liberty that God has in mind for you when He says,

"If the Son sets you free you'll be free indeed!" - John 8:86

He says,

*"**If you continue in my word,*** (in the truth of My gospel, *in what is accomplished and revealed in redemption*) ***then you will <u>know</u> the truth, and <u>the truth</u> will set you free!"*** - John 8:31-32

Hallelujah!

Back to verse 17 of Romans 7,

*"**So then, it is no longer I that do it, but Sin which indwells me**"*

Verse 18,

*"**For I know that within me nothing good dwells, that is, in my flesh …I can will what is right, but I cannot do it!**"*

Verse 19,

*"**For I do not do the good I want, but the evil I do not want is what I do**"*

Verse 20 concludes,

*"**Now if I do what I do not want, it is no longer I that do it, but Sin which dwells within me!**"*

Verse 21,

"So I find it to be a law, that when I want to do right, evil lies close at hand!"

Do you see how Paul discovers here another law or another government?

He discovers that invisible government, that invisible dominion, that invisible nature, that invisible <u>outside influence</u>, *that is now on the inside of him, exercising its control!*

Paul defines that law, or that government, *that invisible dominion* here in the next two verses,

He says in Verse 22,

"For <u>I</u> delight in the Law of God, <u>in my inmost self;</u>"

Verse 23,

"...but I see in my members another Law, at war with the law of my mind, and making me captive to the law of Sin which dwells in my members."

So Paul says now,

'I've been educated through the Law of God, through that law of Moses (...or what I think is the Law of God, through that law of Muhammad, or Buddha, or Confucius, or whatever other religious guru, or societal or political rule of conduct or conscience, or way of thinking I am following and adhering

to, other than Jesus) and my mind has been educated…'

But let's keep it in context here, so Paul says,

'…through that Law of Moses, I have been educated in the Law of God, and my mind has been educated, and my mind has been meditating, and dwelling upon the good standard, the good moral qualities that God has in mind for me;'

He says,

'But alas, I've discovered another law also, and it greatly distresses me. It pains me greatly, because I've discovered that this law is beyond measure, it is called the Law, or the government of Sin, and it works death in my members!'

He says, verse 24,

"Oh wretched man that I am! Who will deliver me from this body of death?"

He was helpless under the Law.

The Law, *no matter how good it is, can do nothing to help him escape the power of this other Law;* **this Law of Sin and Death, this government and invisible dominion <u>with its influence and reign of sin and death</u>**!

But he says in Verse 25,

"Thanks be to God through Jesus Christ our Lord!"

You see, that's why Jesus also challenged the Law. ***In fact, He challenged all religious or societal and political, moral, or conscience law*** *in His teaching* when He said,

"Listen, if your eye causes you to stumble, why don't you pluck it out?"

Why?

*'...**because I find that the very members of my body, designed to be a reflection of God's applause and His approval, a reflection of my design, of me, designed to be the very exhibition of His beauty, of His very own beauty** ...**those very members have now become a stumbling block to me!**'*

*'...**and I find that maybe my only real escape would be for me to escape out of this body or to get rid of every member of my body.**'*

Would that be a release? **Would that be redemption? No it would not be!**

What was Jesus saying then when He said *"...**if your eye causes you to stumble, pluck it out? ...if your hand offends you, cut it off! ...if your tongue offends you, cut it out!**"*

Did He really want us to mutilate ourselves?

No. That is preposterous! Because then you might as well try and go through life blind and deaf and with no hands or feet! Or lock yourself up in a monastery perhaps, like some Catholics do! But as we all can see, that hasn't helped them much either, *especially here lately.*

Ha… ha… ha…

No, Jesus wasn't actually suggesting for us to go and blow ourselves up, like some Muslims, or to lock ourselves up, or chop our hands off, or poke our eyes out, and go through with such foolishness. *He was saying what he was saying* **to expose just how weak the Law was, how weak our religion is, against the power of Sin!**

Listen man, it was not a matter of just trying to get rid of the cobwebs. *It was the spider that needed to be killed or removed!* And so in Verse 25 the last part there, we have Paul's summary, his final testimony under the Law. **If Christ didn't come, then that would have been all that life could possibly be under the Law, under religion.**

"So then, I of myself serve the Law of God with my mind only, but with my flesh I serve the Law of Sin."

What a pathetic existence! What a poor substitute and excuse of a life that would have been! That is what life was under the Law though, ***but now look again at Paul's conclusion in the gospel*** *in Verse 24,*

"Wretched man that I am! Who will deliver me from this death sentence! From this body of death? From this union with Death,

this Law of sin and death? From this power, this invisible dominion over me?"

He says,

"Thanks be to God through our Lord Jesus Christ!"

It's a done deal!

Ha... ha... ha... Amen! Hallelujah!

How can we afford *to keep thinking* like people under the Law, *like Old Covenant people, like people <u>who are still trapped under the power of Sin</u>?* How can we keep living <u>*as if Jesus never came*</u>? I mean, how can we keep living *as if <u>in my mind</u>, I'm going to just be identified with Jesus, <u>but in my body</u>, I'm just going to continue in sin, as if I'm still under Sin?*

Listen, we can no longer buy into that lie and afford to think that way, *<u>trapped in ignorance</u>!*

Chapter 9

Our Identification With Jesus!

We need to read Romans Chapter 6 *as the final release of revelation* **of what our identification with Jesus means!**

Let's quickly look at Romans 6:12,

"Let not Sin <u>therefore</u> reign in your mortal bodies."

Now listen, if Jesus Christ did not deliver us from the power of Sin, *Paul would be asking too much of me here in verse 12*

Can you see that?

Otherwise he would be saying, *'Listen folks, you are going to have to **just try** and get your conduct straightened out! Don't let sin rule in your body, I mean, **just try your best** not to give in!'*

But no, his own experience and testimony has been that, *"The good I wanted to do* (in my own will-power) *I couldn't do, because of the Law of Sin and Death at work in the members of my body."* **So for him now to be asking me to do something** *he himself* <u>**can't do**</u> **is unfair and just plain stupid!**

Listen, the power of the Law of Sin and Death *is broken in Jesus!*

So Paul is not telling us to rely on willpower, *because he knows firsthand what an exercise in futility that would be!*

No, he is sharing and imparting *revelation*, he is imparting the very faith of God *that liberates those who embrace it!*

We are now talking <u>the power of God</u> here; not mere will-power!

He says,

"Let not Sin <u>therefore</u> reign in your mortal bodies."

Did you notice that word, *"<u>**therefore**</u>"?*

Paul says,

"Hey man, I am not embarrassed about the gospel I preach; I am not ashamed anymore! Because it's not like the Law, powerless against sin, but no, it is the power of God unto salvation, wholeness, for everyone who believes."

He says,

*"**It's from faith to faith!**"*

That means: **I no longer have to rely n my own willpower!**

No. The very faith of God is imparted, *and the power of God with it!*

So if Paul is not talking about willpower then what is he saying to us over here in Romans Chapter Six?

He is revealing to us the extent of our redemption!

Look at Verse 17 of Chapter 5. He says, *"If, because of one man's trespass, Death reigned, through that one man, much more, will those who receive* (those who embrace) *the abundance of grace and its free gift of righteousness, reign in life, through the one man, Jesus Christ!"*

So, God, through Jesus Christ, has broken through the dominion of Sin and Death **in order to release you to agree with God!**

Look with me also at Colossians 2:14,

"Having canceled the bond which stood against us, with its legal demands. This He put aside, nailing it to the cross. He thus disarmed the principalities and powers, and made a public spectacle of them, triumphing over them in it!"

Jesus totally disarmed the devil of his ability and his authority to continue his rule over Man, independent of Man's co-operation!

That's why Paul in Romans 6 and verse 11 concludes,

"So you then, must consider yourselves dead to sin and alive to God!"

I keep coming back to these truths over and over again, *so that you can really find them established in your heart.* I have another book also that goes even more in depth into this subject called: *Resurrection Life Now!,* but I don't want you to get your brain all tied up in knots now. *I want you to just read and listen with your heart okay!* This book is really just a brief introduction to the teaching of righteousness and I expound on that subject in almost every one of my books, so you might also have to get and read a few more of my books.

Ha... ha... ha... How is that for marketing?!

No, listen, I am not just advertising my books for the sake of advertising. I really do believe that any book of mine you get your hands on *will help you discover who you are in God's measure of you, and in Christ Jesus. They will help you grow in your understanding of these things,* **and therefore in the freedom in which Christ has set you free!**

So, you might as well get and read them all! ***They will bless your socks off!***

Ha… ha… ha…

And you might just need to come and visit us and spend some time with us in real fellowship, if you really want to be equipped in your understanding and your appropriation of these things for your own life, and for ministry of these things to others!

Oops, did I really say that! Yes, I did, and I meant it too!

Now where was I?

Oh yes ...you see, *the power and dominion of Sin, the power that Sin had, to operate in my life and cause my very members of my body to be an embarrassment to me and to my fellow Man,* **has been broken!** And therefore Paul says ...no, God says, **"We may <u>now</u> consider ourselves dead!"**

And *on the basis of that*, Verse 12 says,

"Let not Sin <u>therefore</u>..."

That's what that **"<u>therefore</u>"** is there for! ***It is referring to the conclusion of the gospel; the conclusion of the work of redemption!***

Paul is referring to that calculation and conclusion made in the previous verse.

Verse 11,

"Considering myself dead to sin;"

"Let not Sin <u>therefore</u>..."

"Let not Sin <u>therefore</u> reign in your mortal, (in your dead) **body."**

(That word *"mortal"* speaks of *"death".*)

"Let not Sin <u>therefore</u> rule in your dead body to make you obey its passions."

Why? Why is my body dead?

Because I can no longer, in all honesty, use my body as an excuse anymore. My body is merely a glove; *a lifeless glove.* It is the hand in the glove *which animates the glove; <u>not the glove itself</u>!* My body is therefore no hindrance to me; *it is no hindrance when it comes to expressing the nature of God, the life of God, the very image and likeness of God in me; the Christ-life; that life-quality I was designed to enjoy and exhibit!* **Because I have come to a faith-conclusion!** ***I have come to the accurate conclusion of my redemption in Christ! I have come to the conclusion that it was a successful redemption! And therefore I have considered my body dead! No longer a hindrance to me, no longer taking on a life of its own, but instead, fully capable of giving expression to every good thing, that is within me, as revealed in Christ Jesus; that very Christ-life that is within me!***

Verse 13,

*"**Do not yield your members to Sin as instruments of wickedness, but yield yourselves to God as people who have been brought from death to life, and your members to God as instruments of righteousness.**"*

*"…**weapons of righteousness**"*

Literally, *"…**weapons of righteousness**",* says the Greek.

Verse 14,

"For Sin will have no dominion over you, <u>since</u> you are not under the Law <u>but under grace</u>."

What does it mean to be *under grace*?

Shall we sin more so that grace may abound?

No!

For by grace I have been saved!

Under grace I am under the gift of righteousness! That means, *I am under the rule and the dominion of a certain life-quality, an endless life source; eternal life ...the very life and nature of God!*

The reign and the dominion of righteousness *is now my rule!*

It rules me!

It's now the rule I live by!

Righteousness rules me!

And so now verse 17 concludes and says,

"But thanks be to God, that you <u>who were once</u>..."

Do you have that *in the past tense* in your Bible as well?

"...you <u>who were once</u> slaves of Sin, have become obedient <u>from the heart</u>..."

Listen, the New Testament teaches *the obedience **of faith**.* There is a vast difference between *the obedience of **faith** and the obedience of **works**.* There is a vast difference between *the obedience of **faith** and the obedience of **willpower** under the Law.*

I have written a whole book about *The Obedience of Faith,* and if you read that one you will see the vast difference and the release that comes through an obedience that is not the result of a law that says, *"You shall not!"* **But instead it is the result of a life t<u>hat releases its energy within me</u> to will, and to do, amen!**

*"…***you <u>who were once</u> slaves of Sin, have become obedient <u>from the heart</u>, to the standard of teaching, to which you were committed.***"*

Hallelujah! No longer obedient *to the standard of the Law,* to that standard of teaching, *that inferior standard,* **but to the standard of <u>revelation</u>, to that standard of <u>truth</u>, and its life-impartation! You are now obedient to that standard of <u>the revelation of grace</u>! The revelation and standard of God! The measure of God! That standard of teaching!**

This teaching in this book and in these Scriptures *is that very standard of teaching that we're looking at!* This measure of God, **this standard of teaching,** *is the mirror-reflection we're looking at!* And it's this measure of God, **this standard of truth, this mirror-reflection, this standard of understand, and of <u>faith</u>,** *that releases us from the dominion of Sin and of sin in our lives!*

Chapter 10

The Glory Of Man Versus The Glory Of God!

Okay, I have gotten just a little bit sidetracked into all that now, just as a little bit of background, but I want us to quickly get back to Romans 3 and *God's measure of us*. We stopped there in Romans 3 verse 23. And we have seen that all have sinned and fallen short of the glory of God.

Let's read it there, Romans 3:23 & 24,

*"...**and since all have sinned and fall short of the glory of God, they are all justified by His grace as a gift, through the redemption which is in Christ Jesus;**"*

The word *"glory"* in the Hebrew is really the word *"weight"*, **something with content, with substance!** That's why Paul who knew the Hebrew, and renewed its meaning for us in New Testament terms, wrote in 2 Corinthians 4:17-18 that,

*"...the slight momentary afflictions, works for us **a glory of exceeding weight, beyond all comparison**."*

*"So we fix our eyes not on what is seen, **but on what is unseen**."*

He was talking about **the truth of the gospel *being confirmed within him and within those who hear and believe and embrace it,*** and that, regardless of personal sacrifice, *the eternal things, God's eternal measure, that gospel of Christ,* **was just getting more and more precious and becoming the very substance that is transforming people's lives.**

He says in verse 15,

*"**For all this is for your benefit, so that the grace that is reaching more and more people may cause thanksgiving to overflow to the glory of God!**"*

You see, we're not looking at the hypocrisy of Man; *Man's alternative glory.* That's why Romans 3:27 says,

*"**What becomes of our boasting?**"*

*"**It is excluded!**"*

*"…**upon what law?**"*

*"…**upon the law of works?**"*

*"**No!**"*

What is the law of works? **The law of performance, or the law of achievement,** *through my own ability*.

Paul says, *"**It is excluded through the law of <u>faith</u>!**"*

The law of faith, that faith of God *cancels Man's alternative glory!* **You see, Man's desire for glory *has made a hypocrite of him!* Man had to escape into hypocrisy *because of his gnawing hunger for positive recognition!*** In Ephesians Chapter Six, Verse Six Paul speaks of a laborer who through eye service *wants to be a Man-pleaser.*

Why?

Behind his boss's back he's lazy, but in front of his boss, boy oh boy, he's trying to be the most diligent.

Why?

Because he's hungry for recognition! And then the boss again also, Paul says, how the boss, through harsh language, wants to enforce his authority.

Why?

He's also hungry for recognition!

And so he is living a hypocritical life, *hiding behind some status symbol!* Hiding behind some kind of qualification that Man approves of, hiding behind his diplomas and his degree; *hiding behind Man's applause!* Living a phony life, but deep inside *he is totally unfulfilled!*

E.W. Kenyon writes in his book, *Two Kinds of Life,* about the corrupt standards of worldly wisdom (and I am not quoting him directly, so you'll have to get his book if you want the direct quotes), but he says, *"**Sense-knowledge has never produced a civilization that it did not eventually destroy! Nor has it come up with a monitory system that did not enslave the masses to false values! Nor has it ever originated and developed an educational system that did not corrupt the spirit of the human being!**"*

Wow, no isn't that something!

Let's go to 1 Corinthians 1 now, and take a look at Verse 26.

Now remember we've looked at Paul's reputation, his identity in the flesh, *and how he at one point considered that reputation as a refuge,* **but how he now considers it as refuse!**

Ha…. ha…. ha…

He considers that reputation he built up in the flesh *as refuse* **in the light of the excellence of the knowledge of Christ Jesus,** *and the excellence of being found in Him* **...to be found in His righteousness and His approval!**

And so he says in Verse 26,

*"**Consider your call brethren;**"*

*"…**not many of you were wise according to worldly standards;**"*

And so he begins to measure the wisdom of this world, and what this world approves of, in terms of their appreciation. He says in essence,

'You who embraced this gospel, look at yourselves, do you remember how you were, you were empty, starving even, desperate and hungry <u>for love and approval</u>, and you didn't have much left, you didn't have a whole lot of pride left, you didn't have much to boast in! Do you remember how you woke up to the emptiness of this world, how it had nothing left to offer you, and how you came to the end of yourself, and you came and you embraced this gospel in humility?'

'…not many of you were wise according to worldly standards, not many of you were powerful, charismatic, talented, or influential, not many were of noble birth…'

It reminds me of Jeremiah 9:23,

"Thus says the Lord: 'Let not the wise man glory in his wisdom, let not the mighty man glory in his might, let not the rich man glory in his riches;'"

Verse 24,

"…but let him who glories glory in this, that he understands and knows Me."

Do you see how the worldly wisdom and its standard had to be and has to be exposed for the deception that it was and is? That's why God the Father and Jesus would choose

(1 Corinthians 1:28), *"…**that which was lowly and despised in the world;**"*

*"…**even things that are not**,"*

*"…**to bring to nothing the things that are!**"*

What are the things that are? It is the things that mankind approves of! **The excellent standards of academic qualifications and ethical conduct** *that humanity as a whole and society as a whole approves of …without listening to their own media and reading their own newspapers, declaring the opposite! Revealing and exposing the moral depravity and the hypocrisy and the poverty of Man's spirit. even among the highest ranks!*

*"…**that which was lowly and despised in the world;**"*

I still remember how often, while doing military service in South Africa, I had to look at, and were absolutely disgusted with, our top military officers. They were top men, the men everyone had to look up to, *becoming absolute pigs at a party! Pigs I tell you! They have the highest ranks in the military, respected by all of society, and here they were, groveling in their own vomit! And 17 or 18 year old youngsters had to follow their footsteps!* **And today I am sure it has gotten even much worse than that! We have accepted the standard this world measures by,** *to be the mold!* **What deception!**

So God despised the lie that was introduced through the government of Sin! ***And He still despises that lie and that deception!*** God despised that deception introduced by that invisible dominion of Sin and of death, and He sent the Law first, and then finally He sent *His own mold;* His *"MONO GENES,"* says the Greek. **He sent His original, authentic begotten, blueprint son, <u>born only of the Father</u> and not of the flesh; not of Sin. And that Son, that mold, that measure, the origin of our being, came in person in the incarnation, *so that mankind's mouth, <u>every mouth</u> could be <u>stopped</u> in our own opinion and our hypocrisy and our own inferior glory and our own measure and our own distorted, fallen identity, and existence, and life-style! So that <u>every mouth</u> could be <u>stopped</u> in our own effort to justify ourselves.***

So that's why the Law came and revealed Sin and it's fruit of sin to be sin beyond measure! But praise God we were not just left with what the Law came to reveal and expose *and yet with no way of escape!* **Praise God, the righteousness of God has been revealed!**

You see, the wrath of God, that which God disapproves of and which disappoints Him, and which deserves lawful punishment according to the standard of the Law, *has also been revealed.* I can measure God's wrath, I can measure through the Law what that term: *'The Wrath of God'* is all about; I can measure **that which God disapproves of and which**

disappoints Him. I can measure it by the Law in no uncertain terms. The Law declares that those who do these things are worthy of death, ***but hey, God has, in Christ Jesus, laid that concept of wrath and of death aside! He has put the concept of the wrath of God as taught through the Law aside permanently when God gave Himself* to release us from the grip of *our transgressions! In giving Himself, he canceled the bond with its legal hold upon your life! He canceled that dominion, which Satan had upon your life, that rule and reign which he exercised within you!* And Jesus did it, <u>by fully representing you in death</u>! When He took away the punishment that was our due, according to what the Law demanded, He took it away <u>by absorbing it into Himself</u>! He died our death! And thus He brought us peace!***

*"…**and therefore being justified freely by His grace, through God's faith** (...through* what God believed happened there in the death of Christ)***, we have peace with God!****"*

And so, our faith now embraces it as reality!

Ha... ha... ha... Hallelujah!

The righteousness of God has been revealed!

God's original authentic measure, God's mold, God's eternal standard of approval and acceptance has been revealed!

God's righteousness, His eternal truth, came in person, in Jesus Christ!

He came in person to redeem us from that against which the Law was helpless!

He came to redeem us from that which the Law could never redeem us from! ...*It wasn't strong enough, because it was never meant for that purpose.*

Father God came personally, in Jesus, and delivered us from the power of the Law of Sin and Death!

He came to set us free from the one who held the power of death: *the devil!*

He came, in Jesus, to display and redeem our original design!

He came to reveal and restore our true identity!

He came to return us to glory!

He came to reconcile us to that truth!

Jesus came to reconcile us to our Father!

God came to replace our glory with his glory!

...To restore us to our original glory, and that original life-quality we were made for, to enjoy with God!

Jesus came to redeem and restore the image and likeness of God in us!

And now the gospel comes to awaken that dormant design in us; *that treasure, in earthen vessels!*

The gospel comes to awaken that full expression of the image and likeness of God in flesh; *in a flesh body* ...*in us!*

So, God chose what is low and despised in this world, **to bring to nothing the things that are.**

"...so that no human being might boast in the presence of God."

Why?

Is God against boasting, *when He Himself fell down upon His knees and boasted in His creation; in Man?*

Is God against boasting, *when He created our very being for His applause?*

No, not at all, **but let him who boasts,** *boast in the Lord!*

Let him glory *in the Lord!*

Listen, **in us, God created a being of such majesty, that He calls all heaven as His witness, to behold the beauty and the glory of what He has placed in us and sees in us!**

He has called all of heaven as His witness *to behold* **the splendor, the flawlessness, the innocence, of a creature, of a being, which reflects His very being and exhibits Him!**

Can you now see why God would be against Man's boasting then, *Man's boasting in the flesh, in himself?*

It's because of the false standard!

It's because Man *does not appreciate* God's true standard; *that original life-quality God had in mind!*

Man does not appreciate God's true measure of Man's being, *but they hold to a false standard.*

God is against Man's boasting, *because of that false foundation Man is building upon!*

It's because of the hypocrisy, *the falseness Man is hiding in!*

Our own righteousness becomes filthy garments!

We appreciate and hold to the wrong measure, *and to an inferior life-quality!*

But, I thank God that verse 30 of 1 Corinthians says, *"Of God are you in Christ!"*

"...Whom He made our wisdom!"

You see, **it's a measure, it's a wisdom *of different kind!* It's a standard of approval of another kind, of another nature! It's a life-quality of another nature!**

"Of God are you in Christ!"

"...Whom He made our wisdom!"

"…our sanctification, and righteousness, and redemption!"

Verse 31,

"Therefore it is written, 'Let him who boast, boast in the Lord!'"

Ha... ha... ha... Hallelujah!

We boast in You Lord! We boast in You Jesus! We boast in what You have revealed! We boast in Your wisdom! We boast in Your measure; *in the measure You have measured us by!*

"Of God are we all in Christ!"

"…Whom He made our wisdom!"

"…our sanctification, and righteousness, and redemption!"

And now I love what Romans 3:27 says. It says,

"Then what has become of our boasting?"

What has become of our inferior life-quality?

"It is excluded!"

It is done away with!

Thank you Papa!

Thank you Jesus!

Thank you Holy Spirit for revealing these things to us!

Chapter 11

There Is No Comparison; No Alternative Will Do!

Let's also go to Psalm 62 quickly and start at Verse 9,

"Men of low estate are but a breath;"

*"…men of high estate **are a delusion**;"*

*"…**in the balances they both go up**;"*

*"…**they are together lighter than a breath**."*

Do you see how desperate this world needs a new standard?

Listen, God wants to pioneer a new standard and a new concept of education!

I thank God *for the home school system,* and for some other minor changes being introduced in the educational systems of this country. I wish I could say a lot of good things about it right now, **but there isn't much worth praising.** There will have to come a whole lot more change before I can even begin to get excited about the educational system we have in this country.

Do you see how mankind, how the whole of humanity, through the development of their

own, and the cultivation of their own civilization, *at the same time is busy digging their own grave?* **In no other civilization in the past has Man ever faced larger moral problems than in this one we live in today! We've never faced larger problems as far as every form of sin and degradation is concerned.** *I don't even have to quote statistics for you to know what I am talking about, because there is enough evidence in every single news broadcast and every blog on the Internet of what has happened to mankind through the Fall!*

And humanity is still trying to build that mask of deception *through their excellence in technology and excellence in scientific breakthroughs,* **and excellence in every aspect of this so called modern age. But we are failing, through that garment of our own making, to hide our nakedness!**

Revelation 3:17,

"For you say that you have become rich and are in need of nothing;"

But God says,

"You do not know your own state, your poverty and nakedness."

"You are wretched, pitiable, poor, blind, and naked!"

Listen; there is no alternative **approval, no alternative applause, no alternative opinion,**

and no alternative appreciation that could ever fulfill *that hunger in the heart of Man.*

Let's quickly go to 2 Corinthians 10:12,

"Not that we venture to class, or compare ourselves with some of those who commend themselves."

On what basis would men be able to commend themselves? **On the basis of *their own* standards!**

Paul says,

"We're in no competition!"

"We who teach and promote the gospel, in our churches and our discipleship schools; we are not trying to compete with the world's standards of education and the world's standards of excellence and compare ourselves with them, so that eventually they think, 'Well, you Christians, you know, you can dress better than us, and you can drive richer and better cars than us, and build larger and fancier buildings and homes...'

Ha... ha... ha... Hey no way man! That will never happen! And if you still think it will, you are fooling yourself!

Listen, *it's a snare man!* Trying to win the world with their own system will never work!

Paul says here in 2 Corinthians 10:12,

"Not that we venture to class, or compare ourselves with some of those who commend themselves."

"But when they measure themselves by one another, and compare themselves with one another;"

He says,

"…they are still <u>without</u> understanding!"

That is why God said about the man who was building bigger and bigger barns in Luke 12, who was probably surely to be elected as the next leader of that community because of his wealth and his excellent achievement and his excellence in business, but God said to him, *"You fool!"*

Why would God say that to such a seemingly successful man?

Because he was in poverty as far as his relationship with God is concerned! He still lived his life trapped in ignorance when it comes to his true identity!

You see, he had a wrong measure of what wealth is!

He had the wrong measure of his wealth, *of his true wealth ...of his true LIFE!* He had the wrong measure of his *life,* ***of life more abundantly, of that specific life-quality God has in mind for us!***

You see, he through no small effort of his own thought to build a big enough barn *to secure an eternal future for him in the natural, and hopefully in the eternal as well,* **but God said of him,**

"This man is a fool!"

Jesus said,

"Life is not found in food and clothing. Life is not found in the abundance of the things you possess!" - Luke 12:15 & 23

And God also says to us here in 2 Corinthians 10:12,

"While we compare ourselves with one another, while we measure ourselves by Man's standard of approval;"

"…we are still <u>without</u> understanding!"

And now Paul says in Verse 13,

"We will not boast beyond limit…"

That word *"limit"* there in the Greek is the same word translated as *"measure"* in verse 12.

He says,

*"We will not boast **beyond measure!**"*

You see, the moment you begin to seek for a measure *beyond God's measure* **you immediately fall back into bondage! Because you inevitably go back to an inferior measure!** You go right back into an inferior measure, *into works and performance, trying to impress Man again!* Trying to impress other people, l*ooking for approval and applause! Looking and searching again for what you already have!*

Paul says,

"But we will <u>keep</u> to the measure (or the exact limit, or the mold) *God has measured us by!"*

What he was saying is that,

"We are determined not to fall into the trap of the church growth programs, and how to compete with this one and that one. We are determined to not get caught up in how to have the biggest church in our area, and how to run our ministry as the world would, as a business, and as a CEO, and how thus to have award-worthy excellence in our ministry, and how to now do ministry in such excellence so as to impress the ignorant Christians and the gullible masses and the whole business and educated prideful world, so that eventually they will all come and join the crowd and attend our meetings, and think, 'Wow, you guys really have your act together, and you really have something to say!'"

No! Nonsense!

Paul says,

"Whatever gain we had in the world and in religion <u>was all pride based and revolved</u>

<u>around our ego</u>; our identity in the flesh, trying to uphold the image we have built up for ourselves to justify our existence and feel important, and gain approval and acceptance. *It all revolved around fame and fortune, power or influence, a never ending perpetual circle, the one feeding into the other, <u>with pride and money at the root of it all</u>.* ***And so now all that we gained in that system now becomes refuse to us!***"

"***Whatever gain we had we count it refuse!***"

"***We put zero confidence in the world's systems!***"

"***But our confidence is in the truth of the message of God!***"

"***Our confidence is in the measure that is of a different quality!***"

"***Our confidence is in an approval of a different kind!***"

"***…an applause of a different kind!***"

"***We will not be in competition with some of those who commend themselves!***"

That's why Paul says,

"***We do not need a letter of recommendation!***"

"***…in order to sell our ministry!***"

He does not say,

"Your life now becomes the means to promote our personal wealth and fortune and fame!"

No way!

He says,

"Your life becomes the vehicle that promotes, not our wealth, but the wealth of God!"

"…That wealth of God has been engraved upon your heart, not through ink, not through the hand of Man, but through the Spirit of God …you have become a living epistle; genuine, sincere, loving people …image bearers of God, with no guile and no hidden motives or worldly ambitions that ruin friendships…"

"Your life becomes the vehicle that promotes the wealth of God!"

"Your life becomes the fruit of the travail of His soul …known and read by all men …an open book of God's grace …a genuine ambassador of Christ Jesus, who has His same heart; His character …true ministers of reconciliation …ministers of a New Covenant!"

Paul says,

"…that is what promotes our ministry and your ministry; that is what promotes the ministry of God; that is what promotes real New Testament ministry! Real ministry is

not promoted by letters of recommendation; it doesn't need it!"

"We are ministers of the reality of the New Covenant, not of the letter, no longer of the Law. For that ministry under death, that legalism with its rules and regulations just kills, man, it kills! But we are ministers of the Spirit, ministers of life, imparting that life and truth and love of God through words …imparting that approval, imparting the knowledge of your righteousness, the revelation of it, deep within your heart, imparting that applause …and imparting that new life-quality, the life-quality God designed the whole human race for!"

He says,

"We will not boast beyond limit – beyond God's measure of us!"

"But we will keep to the limit, to that measure, to the abundant life-quality, God has apportioned us!"

Ha... ha... ha... How beautiful! Hallelujah!

Paul says,

"We will not seek, through compromise, to win someone's favor, so that they can give us a title or a paycheck!"

"We are not looking for, some kind of rank in God's army, thinking, 'Well, at least now I can be a recognized minister or a chaplain. At

least now I have my papers, and I have my credentials!'"

Listen, I really do believe you can do much for God, *by just simply being recognized by Him!* Hey man, don't sell yourself, don't sell your liberty *to Man's alternative; to Man's compromise!*

'Oh, but at least I need a license so I can marry people legally!'

Since when? Not before God you don't!

"What God puts together let no man put asunder!"

Someone needs to expose these things in the Church, in the body of Christ, these wrong attitudes and motivations of the heart, and it might as well be me. If we don't do it, *who will?* **We need to expose these things for what they truly are! *Because we have sold ourselves to a system that has corrupted and ruined the believers, not only in this nation, but now also <u>worldwide</u>!***

Paul says,

"We will <u>keep</u> to the limit, to the measure wherewith God has measured us!"

Hopefully by now you know what that measure is! But you can actually just go ahead and write it in the margin of your Bible there next to 2 Corinthians 10:13. Write there: *Ephesians 4:7 is the measure.*

And what does it say there in Ephesians 4:7?

"Grace was given to each one of us, according the measure of Christ's gift!"

I love what another translation says, it says,

"Grace was given to each and every one of us according to the exact measure of the gift of Christ. Christ himself was the gift! Christ himself was the measure!"

Ephesians 4:7 says,

"Abundant life; a new life-quality, was given to each one of us, according the measure of the gift of Christ!"

There is no other measure other *than the measure of His grace!*

And so Paul appeals in 2 Corinthians 6:1,

"I appeal to you not to receive the grace of God in vain!"

He says in 1 Corinthians 15:10,

"By the grace of God I am what I am!"

"…and His grace towards me was not in vain!"

And he is not saying that as an excuse for poor conduct!

No. He is boasting in the Lord! He is triumphing and glorying as a trophy of grace *in the victory of Christ on his behalf!*

Ha... ha... ha... Hallelujah!

He says in 2 Corinthians 13:8, *"**For we cannot do anything against the truth!**"*

He says, *"…**but only for it!**"*

Chapter 12

The Accurate Measure Of Ministry!

Now look at the strategy of this man, Paul, in advancing the gospel, there in 2 Corinthians 10:13, when he says,

"We will keep to the limits which God has measured us by, or apportioned to us."

And so we think,

'Well Paul, that means, you just stay in Damascus, brother. Damascus is your area, because that's where you got started in the Christian journey.'

Notice, he is writing this letter to the Corinthians, to the Greeks living in Corinth.

And so you can go and study your maps to find out for yourself and see that *there is quite a considerable distance* between Damascus and Corinth **which was bridged,** *not by some clever vehicle or transport of today, not even by the latest mode of transportation during those days,* **but by an urgency of his heart that compelled him!**

He was motivated and compelled to bridge that distance between Damascus and

Corinth by an urgency, a ministry urgency that was much more than just trying to make a big name for himself or trying to become rich through ministry.

He says that a desperate necessity was laid upon his heart to reveal the mystery that was shown him, given to him, and that he was also therefore entrusted with!

That revelation knowledge; that insight into eternal truth, and into the love of Christ was his motivating force; it was the compelling urgency at work within his heart.

And so he says, in the last little line of verse 13,

"…to reach even to you!"

He says,

"There's a large enough measure in my heart, a large enough portion of grace revealed, to include you Corinthians also!"

"There is a large enough measure revealed, for you now to be included also, in the work of grace!"

"…far beyond geographical, or church, or political boundaries!"

He says in Verse 14,

"For we are not overextending ourselves. We are not going beyond the measure of God, as though we did not reach you. We

were the first to come to you all the way with the gospel of Christ!"

Many gospels are preached. **Many versions of it. But Paul understood accurately the gospel of Christ!** That's the gospel Paul preached. He preached **the grace that was given to each and every one of us,** *to the whole human race.* Paul saw them *all* included in his gospel!

"We are not overextending ourselves in reaching you;"

"We were the first to come to you all the way with the gospel of Christ!"

"We came all this way because we saw you included. Otherwise we never would have come. We would never have faced so many dangers to come all the way to you if we didn't see you included in the grace of God!"

"We brought that Gospel to you all the way, holding nothing back, revealing God's truth and love with the utmost clarity, so there could be no confusion left!"

So Paul says in Verse 15,

"We do not boast beyond limit, in other men's labors…"

In other words: *"We don't give them more credit than they deserve! We refuse to be controlled or limited by them! We do not live for their praise or fear their opinions!*

We do not live for them, but for Him who loved us all and gave Himself for us all!"

Who are these other men Paul is talking about?

It is the men he was referring to in verse 12: ***The men who are measuring themselves by themselves.***

Paul *saw no need to be in competition* with Peter, also called Cefas, nor Apollos.

Why?

Because there is only one gospel!

Because they are all sent to proclaim that one gospel!

They are all co-workers, co-laborers, *serving the same Lord!*

They are all undoing the works of a common enemy!

It's the same commission, *the same enemy!*

Paul says,

"We do not boast beyond limit!"

"We do not boast in other men's labors"

"Who they are doesn't matter!"

"It's only the gospel that matters!"

"…the accuracy of that gospel! …Imparting the very truth and love of God in its full measure!"

"All that matters is the one true gospel, the truth of it, the value of Man to God; God's love for all people, which we are all sent to proclaim!"

Paul wasn't concerned about *Man's measure of Paul's life and ministry,* **or Man's measure of the gospel!**

Listen, he did not even care about Man's measure of the gospel he preached!

He did not care about Man's measure at all!

Nor was he concerned about Man's limits!

If he still cared about man-made limits and measures, and about being careful not to offend this one, and, *'Oh, don't overstep your boundaries now brother, and violate So-and-so's space. Don't you know it's their territory, their area apportioned to them!'*

Listen, Paul walked in a lot of love and a lot of kindness and grace, *and he didn't go out of his way to try and offend people. In fact, he tried his best not to offend them. There was no pride in him, no competition, no, us-versus-them attitude. He only had a heart to include them. He loved them and wanted to help further enlighten them as well, and not to come against them, or pit himself against them. He was against no one.*

But let me tell you, **if Paul still** *lived for* **the approval and applause of men,** *for the praise of men, if he was still bound by fear* *of Man's opinion and still respected Man's measure and Man's limits, then Acts 19 would make no sense. I mean, then Paul would have been totally out of order there!*

In Acts 19 Paul comes to Ephesus, and he finds 12 disciples there. They were the disciples of Apollos, who only taught them as far as John the Baptist. Now Paul, if he was still concerned about other men's labors, about limits and boundaries, or any other measure other than God's measure, God's gospel, he would have said, *'Oh, guys I'm so sorry. I really over extended myself now. I pretty much crossed the political boundary, you know, of Apollos' ministry, and I should have respected Apollos more. I mean, I'm in his territory now and ministerial ethics and all that, and I'm so sorry, but now let me correct my mistake real quickly, because I don't want to offend Apollos now. See, I'm going to withdraw immediately and go to Timbuktu, or the jungles of Africa, or something, somewhere where others haven't labored before, because I don't want to boast beyond limits, in other men's labors!'*

No, Paul immediately, when he saw those disciples, *saw their design and identity in God, and he saw their potential in God, to be God's companions and representatives and His ministers also.*

Paul saw these people's ability and potential, to so reflect and exhibit God's image and likeness, and put His grace, that beautiful life-quality, on display in their

lives, and to present that gospel to others also!

And so through those same disciples, it only took between two and three years, but they reached the whole of Asia!

So, now I ask you, did he overstep his boundary?

I think not!

Was he going beyond his limit? Was he going beyond his limit into other men's labors? *Interfering in other men's labors?*

I think not!

He says,

"We went by God's measure; not Man's!"

Ha... ha... ha... Hallelujah!

He says,

"I sow, Apollos waters; but God gives the growth."

"God gives the increase!"

It is not about how large you can measure ministry by in terms of statistics!

Listen Pastors, Christian leaders, *we can never endeavor to measure our ministry in terms of the size of our audience!*

That is not the measure of success!

If you measure success in ministry by the size of your audience, *like so many others do these days,* you will be totally deceived, *along with the rest of their programs you embrace!*

Listen, **your ministry is only as large *as the word you carry!***

If the word you carry is accurate, I mean if it truly is the gospel, then you can speak to the individual *and at the same time include the world!*

Remember Epenetus, the first fruits of Asia?

Paul saw *a continent in a convert!*

Nicodemus ...the woman at the well ...that was the size of the ministry of Jesus!

It may look insignificant to the casual observer, or to the one whose measure of success is the biggest church in town, but I am sure that in the end even they would have to agree with me that Jesus knew what He was doing and didn't miss it when it comes to success in ministry.

Jesus understood the true value of every single individual, and He understood how important it is to minister to people one on one, on an individual basis.

You see, *He saw all the Jews represented in Nicodemus.*

He also saw 10 cities in the Samaritan woman at the well.

...But then shortly and promptly thereafter, in John 6, you can go and read how **they all left!**

Oh how intimidated He could have felt!

He could have felt like His whole ministry was a failure!

He could have felt like a total failure!

But no way!

He never lost a fraction of His ministry, of the impact of His ministry, or the fruit of it, *regardless of who his audience was, or what the size of His audience was!*

The accuracy of the gospel we cherish and represent is *the only measure!*

The size of your audience is never *the measure!*

I say again: **Your audience is never *a measure!***

Do you know what your audience really is?

The utter most parts of the earth! That's who your real audience is! That's the size of your audience!

Ha… ha… ha... Hallelujah!

Now you just go and try to box that into a building!

Ha… ha… ha... No way!

Listen, don't ever be deceived to try and calculate your ministry *in terms of Man's measurements!*

As for you, you'll sit in your prayer closet, in private, *and intimately know the presence of God, and know that you have the world in your hands as you discover His measure of your life, and of your neighbor's life ...as you discover the weight of His glory; of his opinion, restored to you and to your neighbor ...the very glory of God restored in you, and in your neighbor also, through Christ Jesus ...discovering the weight of that glory; discovering His measure for your life.*

Psalm 2:8, says something so beautiful to us who grasp the gospel. God first said it to Jesus, and now He is saying it to us:

*"**Ask Me, and I will give the nations for your inheritance, the ends of the earth as your possession!***"

When that reality, that commission begins to lay a hold of you in your spirit, **then you can even sit in a prison,** like Paul, in fetters and chains, like a criminal, ***because Man misunderstood his ministry; His message.*** But he sat there, **knowing that the word is not fettered in its affect!** *He knew that the word of truth is un-fettered! He knew that the true gospel of God cannot be bound, cannot be restricted, and cannot be* *stopped! It will not go out void! It will accomplish what He sent it forth to do!*

Listen; you cannot put that resurrection life back in the grave!

...And once the truth of the gospel leaves your lips, there is no revering its impact either!

Ha... ha... ha... Amen! Hallelujah!

Hey, ill repute may often come against your life when you proclaim the true gospel, God's gospel, God's version of it, and they will seek to blaspheme you, and seek to close doors, slam them shut even, upon your life and ministry! *But as long as you know God's applause, there is nothing that can limit your life-quality ever again.*

It is the most liberating thing to discover that there is no boundary that can ever limit you or your ministry again!

Ha... ha... ha... Hallelujah!

"We will <u>keep</u> to the measure which God has measured us by, or apportioned to us."

"We will not boast beyond those limits, beyond that measure, thus we will not boast in other men's labor."

2 Corinthians 10:15,

"But our hope is…"

"Our expectation for the future is…"

*"**Our future anticipation, in the light of our now experience, through faith, is**…"*

*"…**our hope is,** (our vision for our ministry is) **that <u>as your faith increases</u>**,"*

*"…<u>**just so, our field**</u> (our impact) **among you,** (and through you) <u>**may be greatly enlarged**</u>!"*

How is that for a measure?!

You see, Paul knows that the real impact of his ministry **can only be measured *in terms of the impact of the truth of the gospel upon the individual's spirit!***

…**And so you see, through the increase of that impact, through an enlarged understanding, the field of ministry will then naturally multiply beyond limit!**

For then Verse 16 also says,

*"…**that we may preach** (through you) **the gospel also in lands beyond you!**"*

Listen; there is no other strategy that God has in mind for our lives and ministry!

There is no other strategy God has in mind for His Church!

There is no other strategy that will work in terms of a global vision *but this one!*

Many strategies will keep you very busy, *but they won't work!*

God's strategy is all wrapped up in His message; *in the simplicity and clarity of His gospel!* *...In the accurate communication and proclamation of it!*

The only strategy that will work is a focus of your life in that message!

...The fruit of such a focus <u>is an impartation of that life you enjoy</u>; an impartation of your life upon the next individual's life!

You see, there is, in that person, the extension of the ministry of Christ *beyond limit!* **...it reaches even into the next generation, and the next one and the next one, and on and on and on!**

...Until the glory of the Lord shall cover the earth as the waters cover the sea!

Now that is some coverage!

Ha... ha... ha...

That is the measure of God!

Chapter 13

Appreciation Always Determines Value!

Would you also quickly go with me to the book of Job and let's look at Chapter Seven, Verse 17. Job is so stricken with a consciousness of unworthiness **because he has wrongly measured the approval of God and the favor of God in terms of his own luxury environment! And so when suddenly there was an absence of material blessings, his innocence was put into question by his friends, *and so his righteousness, his whole identity, and his innocence and approval before God were at stake!***

And so there in verse 17 he asks this question,

"What is Man that You, God, make so much of him?"

"…and that You set Your mind upon him?"

Turn also to the book of Lamentations chapter 4:1,

"How the gold has grown dim!"

"How the pure gold is changed!"

Can I ask you quickly, *wherein lies the value of gold?*

I mean gold is gold, *it doesn't change!*

But what then causes *the value of gold to fluctuate?*

We call it: **Buying power!**

Buying power is determined by *Man's appreciation of the metal!*

It is Man's appreciation that establishes value!

Do you see that if a person is hungry they will trade any matter for their immediate needs? Maybe they've knitted some socks, and their neighbor has cold feet, but their neighbor has some chickens and pigs and vegetables in the garden and whatever, and this guy with the socks is hungry, so they are now going to enter into some trade. **And they measure the value of the transaction *in terms of their own appreciation.***

Appreciation *always determines value!*

One only values what they truly appreciate!

And so it says here in Lamentations 4:1,

"How the gold has grown dim."

Did the gold change, *or did its value change in terms of people's appreciation of it?*

Its value changed based solely on people's appreciation of it.

He says,

"The holy stones lie scattered at the head of every street."

What's he speaking about?

Verse 2 qualifies it and says,

"The precious sons of Zion, worth their weight in gold,"

What is the measure of your life?

"The precious sons of Zion;"

"...worth their weight in gold,"

"...how they are reckoned as earthen pots, the work of the potter's hands!"

Paul says,

"We have this treasure in earthen vessels!"

What is Jeremiah lamenting here?

In the last Chapter of Jeremiah he speaks about how the enemy came in and spoiled and ruined the temple; the very sanctuary.

And so it says in Verse 19 of Jeremiah 52, the second part there,

"...and what was of gold the captain of the guard took away as gold, and what was as silver, he took away as silver."

That means all the beautifully and wonderfully crafted furniture, with all their wonderful prophetic significance *lost their*

value when the glory of God was withdrawn from the sanctuary.

And whatever was left, still skillfully made of gold, was carried away, *as now only worth its weight in gold!*

It now only had natural value left!

But you see, every piece of furniture had a value *far beyond the metal that it was made with.* It had a value as far as God's prophetic word. **Every piece of precious furniture** *was a reflection of what God saw restored to Man.*

And so when the enemy moved in, *the glory of God was already absent.*

"For all have sinned and fallen short of the glory of God;"

But,

"Since all have sinned and fall short of the glory of God, they are all justified by His grace as a gift, through the redemption which is in Christ Jesus..."

You see if we want to discover **the value of our redemption,** *we need to first discover the value of God's estimation of us!*

We need to discover, "What is Man, that God makes so much of us!" ...What is it in Man that attracts the Most High to him exclusively?

If you find that it is difficult to digest all that is being said, *just read it again and keep reading **and listening with your heart.*** You can always read this book again and again *and draw from the word; draw from the revelation.*

I try to make things clear, and I try not to give you too big a piece of steak you can't handle.

Ha... ha... ha... Just messing with you!

But listen, the Church has lived on milk, or worse, junk food *and stuff that has no value* for far too long! So if you find it at first hard to swallow and digest, listen, don't choke man! Relax Max! *Slow down and eat it slowly so you can digest it properly.*

Take what you can and put the rest aside for now, *but don't close your ears* and think, *'Man this is too difficult for me.'* Or worse, *'This can't be right, it must be error. It is opposite to everything my pastor teaches and contrary to everything I have ever believed.'*

Listen, go and study it afresh and new in the Scriptures for yourself if you have to. But whatever you do, **don't shut your ears.** You would be playing right into the enemy's hands because that is exactly what the enemy would want you to do! **Just keep reading, and keep listening with the heart!**

You might have to get some more of my books, or tap into some other grace sources available in written form, or on YouTube, by Francois du

Toit, Andre Rabe, John Crowder, or C. Baxter Kruger *and some of our other mutual friends.*

Just keep studying, and keep reading, and listening *with the heart,* **and you'll soon discover an enlargement in your capacity to accommodate the word; the revelation of the gospel of God and the things being said.** As the word penetrates your heart and settles in your spirit, *you even will find yourself real soon* **speaking the word of truth for yourself; the gospel of our salvation, that word concerning Man's redemption** ...**flowing with it, overflowing with it yourself, without interruption,** ha... ha... ha... **because of the very capacity that the revelation itself creates in your heart for itself to dwell there richly!**

In Colossians 3:16 Paul says,

*"***Let the word of Christ dwell in you, <u>richly</u>, in all wisdom.***"*

That's the measure of the word's indwelling that God requires! ***A rich indwelling!*** **It's the only measure that works!**

Let's turn to Colossians Chapter 1, and I'm going to read to you Verse 5 from the Ruach Translation.

*"**Knowing that you have discovered your hope and dream in everything that was laid up for you in heavenly places.**"*

*"**This was first awakened in you when the truth of the gospel dawned on you!**"*

What was the hope and dream of Man?

...And I'm not talking the American Dream here!

What was the hope and dream of the human race?

Humanity hungers and hopes for a restoration of approval, *they hunger and hope for an applause that would again permanently satisfy!*

They hunger for the approval and applause of their Maker, *of their Origin!*

Humanity hungers and hopes for a restoration to their original design, and life-quality!

And so Paul says that **when the gospel came, that *hope, that experience was again awakened!***

Let me just read to you Colossians 1:19 in the Ruach Translation,

"The full measure of everything God had in mind for Man indwells Him; Jesus Christ!"

The Kenneth Taylor Translation says of Chapter 2 Verse 9,

"For in Christ, there is <u>all of God</u> in <u>a human body</u>!"

We the Church must begin *to study* **Man's glorification in Jesus,** like Jesus talked about in John Chapter 12:20-24.

Do you remember that account of what happened? The Greeks came and said to Phillip, *"Sir we wish to see Jesus"*

Do you know what Jesus' answer was?

He said, *"The hour has come for the son of Man to be glorified!"*

We must discover, how in Jesus, *God totally restored Man to the glory that he fell away from through sin!*

We must also discover how that glory, that image, that opinion of God, has become our portion *through abiding!*

That has become the basis now of every relationship we walk in!

Ha... ha... ha... Hallelujah!

No longer considering Man from a human point of view ...no longer measuring Man in terms of worldly standards, noble birth; the things that matter to Man!

When Paul writes in Galatians about the so called pillars of repute, *the leaders in Jerusalem,* he says, *"****What they are makes no difference to me!****"*

Ha… ha… ha… Now isn't that something.

Listen, who they were, their reputations and so called positions of honor, *made no difference to him,* **not because he was rebellious against so called authority,** but he had a greater respect for the authority of God, *for* *the measure of God.* **He saw those men in that light,** *and refused to look at them in any other way.* **He gave them the respect in Christ they deserve, the same respect we all enjoy, and so he gave them the right hand of fellowship,** *but he did not yield to nonsense, or compromised the truth of the gospel for anything or anyone.*

Why?

He says,

"So that the truth of the gospel might be preserved for you!"

He says,

"What they were made no difference to me,"

"...because God no longer judges Man at face value!"

"What they were made no difference to me."

Because Man's measure of himself and of others and what he thinks the gospel is; *his beliefs, <u>doesn't matter</u>!*

It cannot even begin to be compared to the measure of God!

I say again: **Man's measure of himself** *cannot even begin to compare to the measure of God!*

Ha... ha... ha... Hallelujah!

Praise God!

It is about time that we the Church **start walking in the liberty** *of knowing God's favor and His approval,* which is established upon one law only: *the law of faith* ...*God's faith being imparted to us!* ...*Our embrace of that faith; His faith!*

James calls that law, in James 1:25,

"…the perfect law of liberty!"

He calls it,

"…the perfect law of liberty!"

Or,

"…the law of perfect liberty!"

It's the one and only law, *the one and only truth, which perfectly liberates!*

It's also called: **Our identification with Him** ...**Our perfect identification in Him!**

Ha... ha... ha... Hallelujah!

Thank you my Father!

I bless you Jesus!

Amen.

In closing, I urge you to get yourself a copy of *"The Mirror Bible,"* it is the best paraphrase translation of the Scriptures from the original Greek that I have ever read, and it's available online at: www.amazon.com and several other book sellers.

If you want me or someone a part of our team to come to where you are, *anywhere in the world,* and give a talk or teach you and some of your friends *about the gospel message and these redemption realities,* simply contact us at www.livingwordintl.com …or you can always find me on www.facebook.com

If your life has changed as a result of reading this book, *please write to me and let me know.*

I would love to share in your joy,

…so that my joy in writing this book may be full!

"That which was from the beginning,

which we have heard **(with our spiritual ears)**, which we have seen **(with our spiritual eyes)**, which we have looked upon **(beheld, focused our attention upon)**, and which our hands have also handled **(which we have also experienced)**,

concerning the Word of life,

we declare to you,

that you also may have this fellowship with us;

and truly our fellowship is with the Father and with His Son Jesus Christ.

And these things we write to you *that your joy may be full."*

– 1 John 1:1-4

About the Author

Rudi & Carmen Louw together oversee: Living Word International.

They also travel and minister both locally and internationally.

Rudi was born and raised in the country of South Africa, while Carmen grew up in Cortland, New York.

They function in the ministry of reconciliation (2 Corinthians 5:18-21) and flow strongly with the Holy Spirit and His anointing to teach, preach, prophesy, heal, and whatever is needed to touch people's lives with the reality of God's love and power.

God has given them keen insight into what He has to say to mankind in the work of redemption *concerning the revelation and restoration of humanity's true identity.*

Therefore they emphasize THE GOSPEL, IN CHRIST REALITIES, the GRACE of God, the WORD OF RIGHTEOUSNESS, *and all such eternal truths essential to salvation and living the CHRIST-LIFE.*

They have been granted this wisdom and revelation into the knowledge of God by the resurrected Spirit of Jesus Christ, *to establish and strengthen believers in the faith of God, and to activate them in ministering to others.*

Not only are people set free from the poison and bondage of sin, condemnation and all kinds of intimidation, (upheld, strengthened and reinforced by age old religious ideas born out of ignorance) **but many are brought into a closer more intimate relationship with Father God, as Daddy**, through accurate teaching and unveiling of the gospel message, prophetic words, healings and miracles.

Rudi & Carmen are closely knitted together with many other effective Christians, church fellowships, and groups of believers who share the same revelation and passion **to impart the truth of the gospel to others, so as to impact and transform the world we live in with the LOVE and POWER of God.**

www.ingramcontent.com/pod-product-compliance
Lightning Source LLC
Chambersburg PA
CBHW051837090426
42736CB00011B/1845